# Issues and Challenges

Matters For Consideration, Discussion And Consensus.

Peter C. Bruechle

Copyright 2019 © Peter C. Bruechle
All rights reserved. This book or any portion thereof may not be reproduced or used in any manner whatsoever without the express written permission of the publisher except for the use of brief quotations in a book review.

ISBN 978-0-6485699-4-7

Set in Times New Roman

*To strive, to seek, to find – and not to yield.*
*Alfred Lord Tennyson*


*For peace and continuing development the world needs balanced and comprehensive education, not bigger and more destructive weapons of "defence".*

*Peter C. Bruechle*

# PREFACE.

To understand the background to the following short essays, each of which I have written to stand alone, this preface should be read before the essays are approached. In them I discuss some matters that I consider need review and civilized discussion, and some that I find puzzling. I have provided some thoughts that could prove irritating to those with different points of view. My objective has not been to thrust my own positions down the throats of others but to provide a platform for consideration of the issues. I am not so high-handed or sure of myself that I believe I cannot be wrong. What I want is input from thoughtful people as to how we can assess our existing systems and find ways to improve them, how we can encourage our leaders to concentrate on matters that are important, and to be shown, by better minds than mine, where and why I am wrong, when I am.

I realize that in many of the subjects that I discuss I have joined the annoying ranks of those who consider that because they have raised the problems they have done all they needed to do. They do not propose solutions, possibly because they do not have them, and possibly because if they did propose solutions they could be criticized. I wish I was able to provide answers to some of the questions I have raised. If you find my lack of solutions are an irritant please read the final essay *"Only One World"*. Maybe the problems are insuperable.

Please trawl the index and select those essays that could be of interest.

## ACKNOWLEDGEMENTS.

There have been many people in my life who have taught me and have helped me learn, who have led me to question agreed wisdom, and who have helped me to grow, not least my father. There are far too many to be listed here. I am grateful to them all. Those still alive will know who they are.

Then there are those who have helped me with this book. Thank you – you also know who you are. My special thanks to my wife and to my sons who have edited my writings and formatted this book, and who produced the cover design.

# Contents

Preface. ................................................................................................4
Acknowledgements. .............................................................................5

**Section 1. Religious And Moral Matters.**     **9**
1. Religions..........................................................................................11
2. Life After Death?.............................................................................20
3. The Right To Die. ............................................................................23
4. The Necessity For A Conscience.....................................................26
5. Heroines And Heroes. .....................................................................30
6. Crime And Punishment. ..................................................................32
7. The Meaning Of Life And The Future. ...........................................37
8. Sexuality And Equality....................................................................40
9. Human Arrogance. ..........................................................................44
10. The Motivations Of Humans.........................................................48
11. Rights, Responsibilities And Debts. .............................................54
12. Deceits. .........................................................................................58
13. Honour/Success.............................................................................62

**Section 2. Political Issues.**     **67**
14. Democracy And Its Flaws. ...........................................................69
15. The Political System.....................................................................77
16. Australian Parliaments..................................................................79
17. Being Politically Correct. .............................................................83
18. Money And Financial Rewards. ...................................................87
19. Taxation. .......................................................................................93
20. Complications And Costs Of The Taxation System. ...................98
21. Power, Wealth And The Future. .................................................102

**Section 3. Social Issues.**     **107**
22. Education. ...................................................................................109
23. The Path To Prosperity. ..............................................................112
24. The Creation Of Wealth. ............................................................115

25. The Health System. ...................................................................118
26. Infrastructure And Power Production. ......................................121
27. The Production Of Food And Clean Water. ...............................129
28. The Legal System. ......................................................................131
29. Money. ........................................................................................134
30. Personal Responsibility. .............................................................136
31. Charity. ......................................................................................140
32. The Population Flood. ................................................................143
33. Striving For Wealth. ...................................................................148
34. Inheritance. ................................................................................150
35. Entertainment. ............................................................................154

**Section 4. Art, Architecture And Construction.**                **157**
36. Modern Architecture And Art. ...................................................159
37. Is There A Place For Playfulness In Architecture? ....................168
38. Great Architecture. .....................................................................171
39. The Future Of Architecture And Construction. .........................183
40. Construction. ..............................................................................187
41. Settling Construction Disputes. ..................................................194

**Section 5. Miscellaneous Matters.**                             **203**
42. The Media's Roles And Responsibilities. ...................................205
43. Australia – Past, Present And Future. ........................................208
44. One Australia. ............................................................................219
45. Compensation. ...........................................................................223
46. Reasoning Versus Emotion. ........................................................227
47. Employment For Peace. .............................................................231
48. Humanity's Strengths And Shortcomings. .................................235
49. Equality. .....................................................................................239
50. The Purpose Of Life On Earth. ..................................................244
51. Global Warming – Climate Change. .........................................248
52. Are Humans Important ..............................................................265
53. Only One World. ........................................................................269

# SECTION 1

# RELIGIOUS AND MORAL MATTERS

In this section I discuss some of my views on the important matters of religion and morals. These views will not be to the taste of many because I do not consider that the religious beliefs of many are reasonably based, or that the reason people should behave morally is so that they can achieve everlasting life in paradise. It is necessary, in my view, for humanity to behave in a non-destructive, creative and helpful way so that those now on Earth and those who follow us can thrive on our limited planet.

# 1. RELIGIONS.

I embark on writing about religions with trepidation. It is not a subject that most will discuss quietly, unemotionally and with balance, if they will discuss it at all. For many it is a belief matter, an emotional matter, not an intellectual matter, as I consider it should be. I will try not to offend but only express truths as I think I know them based on what is occurring, what has occurred and what has been recorded.

Since humanity became sentient it has searched for answers to questions that are imponderable. Questions such as why was life created, is there a guiding intelligence that plans our destinies or are we our own controllers, is there life after death or do we simply disappear forever, how should we live our lives and why should we live them in a certain way, will a virtuous life be rewarded, what actions during life are virtuous and what are evil? These are difficult questions and there have been many attempts to arrive at answers.

The early religions I know a little about – the Egyptian, Greek and Roman religions – all had multiple deities led by a head God. Each deity had its own area of authority. The Norsemen also had many deities and a head God. In Japan the Shinto (the way of the Gods) religion, a religion that developed in the 6th century CE, is also devoted to a multitude of Gods. In India the Hindu religion, which has been called the oldest surviving religion in the world, although this is arguable, started to develop about 2500 years ago. It also has multiple deities. Also with its beginning in India was the ancient, and once peaceful, religion of Buddhism with its search for Nirvana. There were many other belief systems with a variety of deities in America, Africa and Australia. The only early monotheistic religions of which I know were Judaism, and the short-lived worship of the sun God Aten by the Egyptian pharaoh Akhenaten. Judaism was based on a relationship, a covenant, between the Israelites and their God.

From this short summary it is obvious that there have been many attempts by humanity to find answers to life's mysteries, and there have been many problems along the way. There is also the matter of the many other religious approaches developed by various tribes. Surely an omnipotent and merciful God would not have allowed this incredible mess to develop and would have stamped His, Her or Its authority unmistakably on humanity. Why would a God intent on uplifting humanity entrust Its message to single prophets such as Moses, Jesus or Muhammad, when It had so many other options? Surely an all-knowing God would have foreseen the shambles that has developed with the world's many religious wars – or did that merciful God deliberately provide the mess for humanity to handle?

The Egyptians with their multiple Gods and their privileged and powerful priesthood, suffered a major religious upheaval when, about 3300 years ago their pharaoh, Akhenaten, attempted to abandon polytheism to worship one God, the sun God Aten. The priesthood revolted because they were losing their power base. They obliterated much of what Akhenaton had built and returned to their many Gods after he died. It is extremely difficult for me to believe the priest's actions were altruistic. Much later, just over 2000 years ago, a Jewish prophet, now known as Jesus Christ in our western world, came forth and announced that he was the Son of God. He started a new monotheistic religion (it is not totally monotheistic as one major branch is led by a Holy Trinity of The Father, The Son and The Holy Ghost). It is now known as Christianity which, after a troubled and persecuted beginning has spread and diversified into several similar but different sects. Then, about 1400 years ago another prophet, a prophet who said he had direct contact with his God through an archangel named Gabriel, unified many of the desert tribes and took over Arabia by force. His religion rivalled and in many cases overcame Christianity and Judaism. His name was Muhammad and his religion is Islam. According to written history Muhammad was not a person of sensitivity or what is now regarded as humanity. He married a six year old, he had many wives, he had many Jews beheaded, he committed rape, he tortured and killed unbelievers and he owned slaves, according to the historical record. Islam took over North Africa and a good deal of southern Europe by force in the following centuries. It took over the Iberian Peninsula about 1300 years ago and ruled it until near the end of the 15th century CE.

Around each of the main religions have been built very impressive displays of architecturally great buildings, distinctive and admiration evoking dress codes for priests, leaders with spirituality, and ceremonies that are aimed at inspiring and appealing to humanity's love of theatre. Attending a religious ceremony in a mosque/synagogue/cathedral with a religion's leading actors playing their holy roles so well, and so effortlessly, is inspirational even for non-believers. The theatre of religion certainly has many appeals.

This, very short, summary of religions is by no means comprehensive, but it is intended to show that not only has humanity been searching for answers for many centuries, it has invented a very large number of beliefs. Each of the monotheistic religions tells its followers that it is the one true religion, which means that all others are false. If only the followers of the one true religion are entitled to a perfect life after death the followers of not only all other religions but all those populations of *Homo Sapiens* that have existed for some 300,000 years, and all those who were not blessed with being subjected to the truth delivered by missionaries from that particular religion, appear to be precluded from enjoying a heavenly resting place. This does not seem to be even vaguely reasonable to my limited engineer's mind. I am not alone.

In about 300 BCE the Greek philosopher Epicurus has been reported as saying, "*Is God willing to prevent evil, but not able? Then he is not omnipotent. Is he able but not willing? Then he is malevolent. Is he both able and willing? Then whence cometh evil? Is he neither able nor willing? Then why call him*

God?" He also said, *"God is all powerful. God is perfectly good. Evil exists. If God exists there would be no evil. Therefore God does not exist."* And that great scientific mind, Albert Einstein, had this to say, *"I do not believe in a personal God"* and he added *"The idea of a personal God is quite alien to me and seems even naïve"*. I am in good company.

In 1543 Copernicus, the Polish astronomer, published his conclusions that the planets, including the Earth, revolved around the sun and that the Earth rotated about its axis every 24 hours. Christians, including Martin Luther and John Calvin, were appalled that an astronomer should consider himself to be more of an authority than God who had said, in Psalm 93.1, *"The earth is established, it cannot be moved."* Copernicus died before he could be punished for his apostasy.

Galileo came to similar conclusions to those of Copernicus and published a treatise in 1632 that led to his indefinite imprisonment by the Catholic Church. Later, towards the end of the 17th century and at the beginning of the 18th century, Isaac Newton developed, among many other accomplishments, such as the development of calculus, the theory of universal gravity. This meant that the universe was vast, that it was controlled by natural forces, and that humanity's home, the Earth, was not being controlled by God. The beliefs of the world were changing. The accuracy of the, God given, Bible was being questioned.

Early in the 18th century, the Spanish Jew Spinoza, who had fled the, Christian-inspired Spanish Inquisition, wrote a thesis that attacked the three monotheistic religions that had arisen in the Middle East; Judaism, Christianity and Islam, entitled *"Treatise on Three Imposters"*, those imposters being Moses, Christ and Muhammad.

For greater detail on the history and beliefs of religions, especially the Christian religion over the centuries, I suggest you read *"All in the Mind – A Farewell to God"* by Ludovic Kennedy.

Despite the cruel history of the three main religions, a history of destruction and what is now regarded as inhumanity in most parts of the world, – (murderous crusades, burning and drowning witches and heretics, cutting hands off thieves, torturing to obtain confessions, killing members of other religions) – and despite conclusions being reached by many superior intellects that religions are based on doubtful contacts between Gods and single men who were not necessarily balanced, that their meetings with the particular God of each have been inaccurately recorded by others well after they were supposed to have occurred, and despite the fact that destruction is still being pursued today by Islam, and is resulting in both Judaism and Christian-led societies carrying out destructive warfare in retaliation, the religions still appeal to many. Why, defeats me. I know that most followers of a particular branch of any religion are almost certain to have been born into that religion or have listened to a persuasive preacher when young, and that they have been indoctrinated into the religion's beliefs at early ages. They are rarely subjected to a comparison of the beliefs of their religion with other religions but swallow, and believe, what they have been told. They can then become concerned that if they do not follow the religion's tenets they will not get the rewards of an everlasting life and the benefits that go with it. If religions educated the young or the susceptible on the beliefs of other religions and of the irreligious I would be less concerned, but given what is being done it is my belief that religious education is virtually brainwashing. It has been said that the Roman Catholic Jesuits believe that if they have the child until he is seven they have the man.

My reaction to the history and diversity of religions is that humanity has not yet found proper answers to its questions and that there is no single religion that is favoured, even if each one thinks it is. They are all constructs of people – either people who have had strange mental experiences or people who have attempted to gain favour or position, and who have gained followers. It is impossible for me to believe that a balanced, thoughtful and all-knowing deity would reveal Itself to only a single person or to even a limited group, so that the present mess of conflicting religions would be the outcome. There can be no single religion that is favoured by an all-powerful God. None of the revelations on which the main religions are founded can have come from such an all knowing, all powerful and merciful God. For more deeply reasoned arguments against the current crop of religions, especially the Christian religion, see *"The God Delusion"* by Richard Dawkins.

The question that has troubled me since I first heard it asked is – with what are we to replace religion, which offers support to many, if we do away with it? And then there are the corollary questions – have religions done more good than harm and are they continuing to be an advantage or a disadvantage to humanity? My own view is that the need for humanity to worship a religion or a God has passed and that religion now appears to me to be destructive of people living together peacefully, as exemplified by the horrors of the Muslim killings. Others, especially those sustained by a religion or who are made to feel superior because they belong to "the only true religion", will disagree with me, but I hold to my view.

The history of some of the important religions, especially the Christian and Muslim religions, is littered with atrocities being done in their name, or being done to a particular religious group because they are easily identified, and atrocities are continuing to be done in the name of Islam (Submission to God) to the present day.

The Christian religion spawned the brutal Crusades, the infamous Spanish Inquisition and the corruption of Pope Alexander VI (Rodrigo Borgia), his children Cesare and Lucretia, and others, when Columbus was discovering the New World. The Old Testament is loaded with commands from God to wipe out other tribes (read Joshua). These activities in the name of Christianity are all well documented. There is also a history of vicious persecution of Christians from early Roman times until the present day. Christianity has now divided into many sects that have formed since the reformation, during which some of the excesses being practised by the Roman Catholic Church of the time were condemned by the reformers. Today there is no militant group that believes in spreading the word of its Christian God by force so that, although there is certainly corruption in parts of the Christian religion, it is generally corruption of, and by, individuals, and is justifiably condemned by the churches when it is uncovered. However a Christian history that I regard as immoral, and a God who commanded his anointed to murder others, are part of Christian heritage.

The Moslem religion, which its adherents claim is a religion of peace, conquered most of northern Africa and southern Europe in the 7th century

CE by force of arms, and imposed its will on the conquered peoples. Today its two main sects, Shiites and Sunnis, are busily destroying each other and destroying ancient monuments in the name of the God of each. Many of their religious practices are quite revolting and their treatment of women can be appalling.

Many of the followers of the various branches appear to be happy to die in the service of their particular religion on the basis that they will receive rewards in the afterlife. I wonder how many would make that supreme sacrifice if they believed there was no afterlife. Many of those who follow the religion believe the Qur'an is the word of their God, that it is immutable and that it has to be followed. I find this frightening. As an example I quote from a translation of Sura 47. In part it says *"When you encounter infidels strike off their heads till you have made great slaughter among them, and of the rest make fast the fetters"*. There are many similar nasty invocations in the holy book of this religion of peace. Recently I was sent a video of very young Moslem boys – not young men, boys – singing about fighting the Jews, carrying out jihad for a world caliphate, and wanting to be suicide fighters. If this is Islam I am vehemently opposed to it and what it is teaching the young. Education that is not balanced is brainwashing of the young and can be, and is, evil.

So religions are likely to be the inventions of hysterics and importance seekers, as logic indicates them to be, but it is religions that have provided much of the moral framework of our civilisations, for good or ill, of both past and present societies. Religions that promise damnation to sinners and everlasting life, or reincarnation, or even 72 virgins for those who have obeyed its tenets, have been a powerful influence and have helped maintain equable relations in the densely populated 'civilisations' that have grown out of agriculture and the husbandry of animals. Religions still have a major influence on the lives of many and affect how many behave. To see devout Roman Catholics emerging from their masses with shining eyes, determined smiles and with their understanding of their place in society and their duty to that society, to see men with ringlets and with homburgs in hand knocking their heads on Jerusalem's Wailing Wall, to see Moslems assembling to their muezzin's call, kneeling and bending to pray, and to see the fervour of Martin Luther King Junior as he leads his dedicated congregations, makes it clear that religion still plays a major role in the conduct of a large percentage of the population of the world.

So I repeat the question – if the bases of religions are false and we want to do away with them altogether, if humanity decides to consign the current monotheistic religions to the bin of history, as the many Gods of Egypt, Greece, Persia, Rome, India, China, Japan and the Norse countries have been consigned – with what are we to replace them?

There is no doubt that some of the world's Christian religions are under attack, are suffering from scandals both from within and without, and are losing favour with many of their previous adherents. The division in the Moslem religion between the warring Shiites and Sunnis is hurting that religion in the Middle East, and in the west of its country communist (?) China is suppressing the Moslem Uighurs. There are major differences between Moslem countries and other countries that could lead to further armed conflict. The non-religious countries, dominated by dictators or communist leaders, are growing in strength and are threatening peace. Africa, with its rapidly growing population and its many poorly led countries, is in an ever-increasing mess. Now Sweden, a bastion of effort and peace, that has accepted Moslems into its society, is suffering from Moslem uprisings, Moslem insistence on sharia law, and Moslems taking control in some areas so that they have become 'No Go' areas for Swedish citizens and the Swedish police force. In Spain, a Spain that has accepted many Moroccans; in France which accepted a large percentage of Moslems as citizens; in Germany who graciously took in many Moslems from troubled areas and now has right wing factions objecting; and in England, where the welfare system encourages large Moslem families, murderous atrocities have been carried out by Moslems in the name of Allah. The globe is troubled. Is there an answer?

There does not appear to be much doubt that humanity needs a new philosophy, a new guiding light. Maybe another mystic will appear and will gain a following as Christ and Muhammad have done, but in today's world of the instant spread of news that is doubtful. Maybe a superior human being or a group of superior human beings will put together a code that the disparate world will gradually come to accept, and abide by, without the promise of a perfect existence after death, but with the promise of gradually improving the conditions under which we all live. Maybe education will make clear that religions have brought about much of the trouble experienced in the past, and at present, so that people will abandon some of their destructive doctrines. Maybe education of all in the different beliefs that the major religions hold will throw up their differences, and will lead to agreement that all are flawed. Maybe humanity's nature is such that peace and progress are not what is really wanted, that acknowledged superiority of an individual's tribe, race, religious belief or sect is worth strife, death and destruction – as Hitler believed – and that fighting and dying for what is believed to be the truth is really what is preferred. If that is so humanity is likely to be doomed to destruction. I hope that intelligent discourse will win the day, but I am not optimistic. Watching Kim Jong-un and his attendants joyfully applauding the success of North Korea's intercontinental missiles and seeing the destruction and death in the Sudan, and in places such as Raqqa, does not give me much hope.

What we possibly need is for an incarnation of Moses to bring down a new set of Commandments based on reason, humility, justice, and the need for humanity to understand that it must behave reasonably, not for a comfortable everlasting life, but to improve conditions on our globe for all and for our future generations. If we cannot arrive at a universally agreed code of conduct, if we cannot put our disagreements behind us, if we cannot agree that the destructive elements of our religions have to be done away with, and we cannot stop the silly posturing of tyrants and leaders with access to frighteningly damaging weapons, the alternative could well be the destruction of the naked ape and the clearing of the Earth for the development of a new life form. The situation, viewed as dispassionately as I can view it, seems to be universal, balanced education and agreement on a universal code of conduct, or mutual destruction. The choice is still humanity's to make.

## 2. LIFE AFTER DEATH?

Life, as someone once said, is a sexually transmitted, terminal disease. Life is certainly temporary. This has led inquiring minds to ask – does life have purposes, and if it does, what are those purposes? Humanity's sense of self-importance does not allow us to conclude that we are just an accident and that we are therefore as purposeless as the dinosaurs, as I think we are.

The question of purpose has been pondered by intelligent beings since humanity began to think, and to question. Despite a number of answers having been developed, it is still not answered to the satisfaction of all. Those answers that have been the most popular and long lived are the religions, of which there have been many – so many that the number alone makes it certain that they are all constructs of the human mind, and that none is God given.

The basic thesis for most religions is that there is a supreme deity or a group of deities that keeps a record of the way in which each person conducts himself or herself (or itself given the present politically correct thrust to deny that a person's physical characteristics necessarily determine masculinity or femininity), during that person's short lifetime, and then makes decisions as to how that individual will be treated after death. Those who behave in accordance with the tenets of their particular religion are rewarded with an existence after they die that is fulfilling, disease free, comfortable and eternal. (would such an existence finish up being boring?). Those who do not obey the religion's rules either suffer in purgatory or are denied eternal life. Religions can even offer after-life rewards of sexual license and alcohol for the righteous. Some believe life is cyclical and that the dead return in different forms. There is a widely held belief that each individual possesses something called a soul, which is an essence of the individual that lives on after the body expires. To an analytical engineering mind these are highly unlikely theses with insuperable problems.

The first question is – if the soul is immortal where has it been prior to finding a person to which it can attach itself? The second question is – when is the soul fully formed? Does it arrive fully formed at conception or at birth? Does it alter according to how persons conduct themselves during their lifetimes, or is it always constant? Does it develop as the character of the person develops, or is each individual stuck with the soul first foisted on him, her or it? The next question is – why are only humans given the benefit of a soul? Why do sharks, jellyfish, elephants and even amoeba not have one? Surely selecting only humans for such a wonderful gift as an everlasting soul is not the act of an all knowing, all seeing, merciful deity?

Another question is – do the souls of crazed people who commit terrible crimes because of brain malfunctions get given a second chance, or are they condemned to purgatory? What about the humans who were never exposed to a religion in the very long period before the present religions were invented? Are they banned from everlasting life in paradise only because they were not fortunate enough to be born after Moses, Jesus Christ or Muhammad? And the 'savages' who lived before missionaries arrived to spread the word of God – are they banned from everlasting life of the soul because of their unfortunate timing?

As any reader will see, it is impossible for a soulless engineer to accept current religious beliefs, especially those that encourage domination by force. How can anyone, except those deranged by a brain washing and unbalanced religious crank, seriously believe that killing others, fighting wars against people of other religions, or bringing down Yamasaki's twin towers in New York and killing thousands, are acts that will result in everlasting life in paradise? The purpose of life, if there is one, remains a mystery for me, but it is not to achieve paradise. What each of us should do is to try to treat others fairly and try to give more than is taken – not for a reward in paradise but because that is reasonable behaviour and because all will benefit, including the giver.

# 3. THE RIGHT TO DIE.

All animals and plants, including us naked apes, die. Our Earth is probably already overloaded with people, so it is just as well that death is inevitable. Given this why does humanity, especially sections of humanity that are prosperous, go to incredible lengths, lengths that involve much human effort and expense, to avoid a terminally ill or terminally unhappy person dying, even if that person has asked to die? The matter of deliberately taking one's own life is clouded by quite unreasonable emotions and what I regard as some weird beliefs humanity has managed to invent. (See *"Life after Death"*)

The debate we should be having, in a reasoned manner and devoid of emotion or clouded by religious beliefs, is do people have the right to take their own lives and, if they are terminally ill and incompetent, should a tribunal make that decision for them? If a person decides that their life is not worth living for any number of reasons (continuing acute pain, chronic lack of mobility, lack of control of bodily functions or even prolonged and excessive sadness or ennui) why should that life be prolonged? Why should a person tired of life be forced to continue to live it? Why should it be illegal to help someone who wishes to die to painlessly pass away? What right has society to make a decision to keep alive someone who has decided they want to die? With whom should the decision lie?

An argument that is advanced against allowing people to die peacefully on demand is that it is now possible to make the severely ailing comfortable so pain is not an issue. This argument overlooks the mental pain suffered by those who have been active and are reduced to immobility, by those who have been impeccable in their personal habits and have lost control of their bodily functions, and of those who have periods of understanding interspersed with periods during which their minds lose rationality. It also overlooks the cost to society of tending to those in a moribund state, and although this is not a primary matter it is certainly one that should be taken into consideration. Spending community effort keeping alive someone who wishes to die seems unreasonably, even stupidly, wasteful.

Another argument, and one I consider to be irrational, is that life is a gift from God and only God should take it away. As God has, apparently quite happily, watched many die of starvation and in Hitler's death camps, seen the butchery on battlefields and overseen the murderous regimes of Pol Pot and other despots, I cannot see how He, She or It can be upset by someone dying peacefully after having asked to be able to do so.

A further argument is that once euthanasia (the good death) is legalised, unscrupulous people will start using it to kill unwanted relatives, sometimes in order to gain property from the ailing. If a death is required to be sanctioned by the person concerned or by a tribunal, this real possibility should not be an issue.

There are certainly lives that are not worth living. If an individual living such a life wishes to continue with it there is no doubt that they should be encouraged to do so. The decision as to who lives and who dies must be the decision of the individuals concerned, and should only be taken from the individual in cases where that individual is not able to make a decision. Then, and only then, should a tribunal be called in to make a decision. This could be described as a heartless procedure but it is the best I can think of.

For centuries humans have made decisions to kill other humans and they are continuing to make those decisions. So why is it regarded as immoral, and in some cases illegal, for a person to ask for a painless death or for a panel to decide that a peaceful death is the best outcome for someone ailing physically or mentally?

Humanity, even Christian humanity, shoots to kill or maim in wars, drops bombs that destroy and kill non-combatants, and daily kills other animals for food. and even for sport, without turning a hair. The Moslem Qur'an says it is a justifiable duty to behead infidels, and individual Moslems and groups of Moslems have no compunction about using weapons or vehicles to kill and maim innocent bystanders. Yet this same humanity baulks at allowing individuals to make up their own minds as to whether they live or die.

It is my view that the decision belongs only to the person whose life is affected, not to anyone else, except when the person is not capable of making a decision. In that case the decision should be left to a tribunal of disinterested parties who have an instruction that if there is any doubt the ailing person is to live.

Society should be prepared to provide a painless death for those who are in a position to ask for such a death and for those who a tribunal, having considered all aspects of the case, has decided that the person is better off dead. I do not agree with keeping alive and prolonging the suffering, either physical or mental suffering, of those with no hope of living a normal life again, unless those persons want to be kept alive. The only beneficiaries of keeping alive a terminally ailing person who wishes to die, are those paid for the services required to keep the person alive.

I realise that my position will be regarded as heartless by many. I find it quite strange that those who are happy to collude in mercy killings of animals do not apply the same logic to suffering people.

# 4. THE NECESSITY FOR A CONSCIENCE.

I was recently told that the wife of a well-known, now deceased, successful entrepreneur, said that he had no conscience, and it started me thinking about conscience. What is a conscience? How important is it to have a moral conscience? Have the great persons of history all had consciences? Are moral consciences a necessity? Are they beneficial? Before we select a person as a leader should we try to establish whether or not that person has a moral conscience? I decided to briefly explore these questions.

According to my Concise Oxford English Dictionary, conscience is *"a person's moral sense of right and wrong"*. The Cambridge English Dictionary says *"Conscience is that part of you that judges how moral your own actions are and makes you feel guilty about bad things you have done or things you are responsible for"*.

Does everyone have such a moral sense, and a guilty conscience when they play a dirty card? To me conscience appears to be a faculty of being able to put yourself in the shoes of the person or persons with whom you are dealing, to be able to see their point of view, and to understand the pain that they could experience from your actions. Surely the mass murderers of history and those who spend their lives taking from their societies would not behave as they did, and do, if they had consciences that judged how immoral their actions were. Are the consciences of some so skewed that what most of humanity would regard to be appalling behaviour, they find to be acceptable?

Alexander, who is still known as 'the Great', took over his father, Philip's, Macedonian throne when he was 19 years old by having his rivals for it murdered. His army then invaded the Greek state of Thebes, where he had all the males slaughtered and enslaved all the women and children. He then invaded Asia. He was obviously driven by a will to win at all costs and had an absolute disregard for those slaughtered and enslaved. Why has history given him the title 'Great' when he was obviously a murderous thug without a moral conscience that troubled him, as most are troubled by vicious acts?

Napoleon Bonaparte saw himself as a latter day Alexander and had no compunction in sending his armies into terrible battles. His armies were successful in many of those battles and he is still lauded as a great general. When he attacked the Russians they allowed him access to their country to stretch his supply lines and awaited what became a vicious winter, which saw his troops massacred. He was then sent into exile on Elba. That would have been enough for anyone with even the least moral conscience, but he came back, resurrected his army, and fought again at Waterloo where Arthur Wellesley's troops, and the Prussian general Blucher's cavalry, narrowly defeated him. He was responsible for thousands of deaths. Today he would be called a war criminal. Surely he could not have had a moral conscience.

More recently the world was subjected to the rise of another conqueror – the Austrian, Adolf Hitler. He and his followers attempted to annihilate entire races of people – the Jews and the Gypsies – and to conquer the European world to prove the superiority of the Germanic race. Surely this man and his band of immediate followers would not have done what they did, and been responsible for the ill treatment of conquered countries, their destruction of cities including their own cities in retaliation, and their attempt to wipe out the Jews, a group of people who have contributed so much to human knowledge, had they had moral consciences. There was obviously something missing in their make-up. They considered that their actions were justifiable, and that the superior Germanic people had every right to rule the world.

From the history of these leaders it is apparent that good leaders need to have moral consciences if they are to lead in a reasonable manner, but from history it is clear that most famous, historically lauded leaders, including those already mentioned and others such as Genghis Khan, Julius Caesar, Muhammad, Mao Zedong and Josef Stalin, have not had the moral judgement necessary to provide balance to their actions, yet they are still revered in many quarters. And today we have other leaders who appear to have no moral compass - Kim Jon-un of North Korea and Robert Mugabe of Zimbabwe are examples.

From this unhappy history it seems clear that when leaders are being selected they should be first checked to see if they are able to assess the morality of their actions – whether or not they have a moral conscience. Unless leaders can judge their own actions they should not be allowed to set the rules for others. This rule should not only apply to the leaders of countries but also to the leaders of industry. Obviously those who lead others to death and destruction are those who most need a moral conscience, but the rule that a conscience is necessary should also apply to those who lead businesses. Unbridled greed, viciousness, personal vindictiveness and a lust for power are appalling but they are often the driving forces of those in charge of countries or businesses. When leaders are being selected qualities that should be checked are – do they have a suitable conscience, do they have morality and balance? Is the person able to examine her or his actions and decide if they are morally right or wrong? If they are found not to have that faculty but are driven by other forces they are not fit to lead, in my opinion. We might still consider the conquerors of the past to be heroes or war criminals and place them on pedestals or bury them in opprobrium but surely we should now be mature enough to make sure our leaders have consciences. Does Donald Trump have a moral conscience? Does Erdogan? Does Putin? Does Xi Jinping? Does Kim? Did Turnbull? Does Morrison? Does Shorten? Or are these leaders driven by an ambition to be in charge – surely not a character trait for sound leadership.

It is also my opinion that morality and the reasons for it being necessary should be a part of normal education. It is exceedingly important that people understand what is reasonable and what is not. A code of reasonable conduct should be part of a normal education. This is not a plea for doing away with rivalry or competition, they can bring out the best in us, but I am against people acting in a manner that gives them some short term gain – whether physical, moral or financial – at the expense of others. I also want to see the game of life played as fairly as possible. If everyone had a moral conscience and understood the damage that was done to both themselves and others by immoral acts, the world would be an easier place in which to live. Based on history this will not happen, and persons with no moral compass or with consciences that are badly skewed, will continue to lead others into destructive nastinesses.

## 5. HEROINES AND HEROES.

Who are the real heroines and heroes of our society? We are all born with certain innate physical and mental capabilities that develop as we grow and mature, and then deteriorate as we age. Some are given strong and athletic bodies, some have high intelligence, and some have few advantages except the advantage of life. The circumstances into which each individual is born play a hand in how that individual develops. Some are provided with many advantages – a supportive family and environment, an attractive personality and appearance, an ample food supply, comfortable living conditions, the opportunity for a balanced education, and a peaceful community in which to live. And some do not have these advantages. Given this matrix of possibilities, who are the heroines and heroes? Who are those to whom accolades and honours should be given?

Should public honours be given to those who achieve fame? Should actors who are idolised because they can portray characters other than their own be given further awards? Should those who have sporting ability, or those who are good looking, those who can write or paint, and those who deliberately seek fame, receive honours or should they be given to those who make the most of their limited talents?

Success in any field should be reward enough without awards being given for being good at hitting or kicking a ball, for being able to afford a fast yacht, for being well known or for being one who can entertain.

Surely those who deserve accolades are not those who publicly succeed but those who quietly contribute to their society as best they can. The real heroines and heroes are not those who aim at high honours but those who work to improve their society. They are those who provide services to their communities and use their, sometimes limited, capacities to the full for the good of those communities. The true heroines and heroes are the quiet achievers, those who try hard and contribute without expecting much in return. The community they serve should let them know that they are the heart and soul of that community – they are the real stars. Or has Australia lost its understanding of where its heart and soul really is?

# 6. CRIME AND PUNISHMENT.

I approach the topics of crime and punishment with caution. The questions of what constitutes crimes, and how transgressors should be treated, are matters that have varied a great deal throughout history, and between social groups. Societies and religions have laid out various boundaries as to what is acceptable, what constitutes a crime, and what punishments or treatments are to apply for crimes of various types. What are regarded as heinous crimes in some parts of the world, and at some stages of history, are treated as quite normal in different times and at different places. Burning or drowning witches has gone out of fashion. Killing or incarcerating homosexuals is no longer the punishment meted out in Western societies. Blaspheming is a crime only in certain societies. W.S. Gilbert summed it up when he wrote, *"My object all sublime, I shall achieve in time, to let the punishment fit the crime, the punishment fit the crime"* for *"The Mikado"*. What are regarded as barbaric punishments for crimes in some societies – chopping off hands, stoning, beheading, whipping, torturing, and hanging – have been and are regarded as normal punishments in other societies.

There are those who consider that the punishment for a crime should be severe enough to act as a deterrent for any who might contemplate carrying out a similar crime, and there are those who consider revenge balances the books, and that justice is done when vengeance is carried out. On the opposite side of the ledger there are those who believe that crimes are carried out by people with unfortunate backgrounds so they should not be punished but should be rehabilitated. These people believe that revenge, often couched as 'justice', is not the path civilised societies should take.

Then there are those who consider that those who damage society should repay their society by contributing in some way. I tend to agree with this approach. I think that the present system in western democratic societies of locking criminals into comfortable gaols at huge expense is foolish. Convicted criminals should be expected to produce food, goods or services that are useful to their society. Gaols should aim at being zero cost institutions. This not only reduces the burden on the public purse, it gives those convicted of crimes a reason for living and the opportunity for atonement.

As you can see, I am unsure as to how criminals should be punished or treated. Most of the time I lean towards the soft approach of rehabilitation and education, of expecting them to pay their society back in some way, but then I hear of a brutal rape, murder or prolonged torture and I think that the only reasonable response is a painless death for the person responsible. That person has outlived his or her reason for being.

There are, of course, various levels of criminal activity and they should be dealt with differently.

The first, and in many ways the worst, are crimes against persons. There is a wide range of such crimes, from deliberate homicides, deliberate physical damage, accidental homicides, accidental damage, rapes, physical molestations of various types and other assaults. And now there is a growing list of verbal offences. (See *"Being Politically Correct"*).

On what bases are the punishments for the range of crimes against persons to be established? A theoretically possible basis of punishments for crimes of physical violence is that they should reflect the suffering that the victim experienced. Because inflicting pain on wrongdoers is now generally regarded as bestial in western societies this is no longer an option. In western societies at this time the normal punishments for crimes against persons are long terms of incarceration in reasonably comfortable gaols complete with balanced diets, exercise facilities, personal cells and good plumbing, all at the expense of the society that has been degraded by the action of those gaoled.

Although I agree that there is no place in a reasonably civilised society for physically damaging wrongdoers I wonder if removal of fear of physical punishment has not led to an increase in gratuitous violence. How those who commit physical damage on others need to be treated must be considered and the most appropriate treatment decided. Do we follow an eye for an eye, or do we rely on rehabilitation? Which approach would be the most successful – the nastiness of subjecting the wrong doer to physical punishment, or the humane approach of re-education? Can those who have a violent nature be turned into honourable and productive citizens? Can vicious murderers be turned around by kindness, or will the kind approach be regarded as weakness and lead to further vicious acts?

These are matters that should be considered and balanced decisions made. My own view is that only by the whole of society having a balanced education that teaches the benefits of contributing to society, and an education that brings out the best in all those who receive it, will society become the useful and peaceful place it has the potential to be. But, and it is a big but, education will only be successful when people want to learn.

My next area of discussion is psychological damage and how it can be dealt with. As with physical damage, there are various levels of psychological damage. My present view is that unless this damage, which appears to be becoming a burgeoning source of income for the legal fraternity in western democratic countries, and is gaining more and more publicity, is accompanied by physical abuse, it has already gained a much higher level of importance than it should have. It is being used as a gag on free speech and as a means of gaining unearned monetary rewards.

This is not to say that I condone making slanderous or libellous statements about others. There are, I understand, already laws that can be employed to deal with such cases. And I do not condone making false statements, but truths, even hurtful truths, have to be borne by those at whom they are aimed. I also think private lives are private matters, and who is bedding with who is not a matter for public opinion or condemnation. Only the stupidly prurient gain anything of value from public exposure of such matters.

I am astounded that in Australia people whose 'feelings' have been hurt can claim money (although it is not called money – it is called the much nicer term 'compensation') and these verbally wounded persons are backed by laws inhibiting free speech, psychologists and psychiatrists, and a growing cohort of the legal profession only too anxious to pursue a dollar. To me it appears to be a waste of legal time and talent, and it adds nothing to our society's wealth or welfare. How words can push any balanced person into a psychiatric condition is beyond me, and those already in such a condition need treatment, not money. For an insult to wound it must have truth and if it has truth it has to be borne.

Now I come to the crime of stealing. Civilisation is based on personal ownership. Without ownership there is chaos. Societies that have attempted public ownership have foundered or have reverted to having private ownership. The supreme current example is China, a communist country awash with billionaires. Even those in the past who were not civilised, the hunters and gatherers and the nomads, had ownership of their animals, their weapons and their tents. It is the owners of buildings and of artefacts created by artists and craftsmen, who nurture them. Societies that do not value ownership do not take care of anything, so nothing is looked after. Without ownership, fair and lasting civilisation is not possible. This means that the stealing of property or money is an attack on civilisation so it is a serious crime.

How should a thief pay the debt owed to civilisation? The basic response should be that the thief replaces what was taken with a margin for the hurt that was suffered. This is not usually possible because thieves are not normally producers of wealth, art or property, so they are not in a position to repay their victims. Instead they are locked away from society in buildings built at the cost of the society in which they have operated, and then fed, clothed and housed in relative comfort, again at the expense of the society they have damaged. Is this a proper retribution for attacking the society in which they live? Is a more justifiable punishment possible? Is it enough to dissuade potential thieves from carrying out their crimes? Are there other possibilities that would more closely meet Gilbert's aims of the punishment fitting the crime?

Of course there are many levels of thievery from the petty, where a poor person steals property or pilfers money, to drug-addled persons who steal to support their habit, to thrill seekers who steal expensive and treasured vehicles and thrash them knowing that the punishment is not going to be onerous, to high level manipulators who steal from their society to support extravagant lifestyles – and there have been many of these in Australia.

It is my experience that those who take from their society without contributing in equal measure are often pleased with their notoriety, their properties, their wealth and their publicity in the media, which is always looking for important figures to feature, but that they lack the fulfilment of those who have gained their livelihoods from contributing in competitive markets. Society needs to make it clear that competing is healthier and more satisfying than stealing or taking more than has been earned. That should be part of normal education. Also, part of any rehabilitation should be that thieves should be made to contribute to the welfare of their society by producing things of value or helping deal with the detritus of society so that they can learn the satisfaction of doing so. And they should be given mandated education on how civilisation is dependent on ownership. I realise that such lessons will probably fall on many deaf ears but if it gets through to even a few it will be worthwhile.

If society is to continue to punish wrong-doers by locking them into expensive gaols it should also attempt to make those gaols productive areas so that society benefits, and the criminals can learn and earn some self-respect.

# 7. THE MEANING OF LIFE AND THE FUTURE.

Since humanity became sentient and began to think, it has wondered why it has life, how it came about, and its purpose. Out of humanity's quest to find answers to these questions have come many answers – most of them based on all-knowing deities who, through selected prophets, have given instructions as to how we are to behave in order to achieve everlasting life, although Hinduism, which often claims to be the world's oldest religion with some justification, is based on reincarnation and, eventually, Moksha (freedom from the cycle of death and re-birth).

Around religions have grown vast organisations and great and impressive edifices that demonstrate to followers how powerful they are – the statues, temples and pyramids of Egypt, the beautiful shrines and temples of China and Japan, the great mosques of Islam in many countries, impressive synagogues, the wonderful and elegant churches and cathedrals of Christianity, and the ornate temples of the Hindus are examples. And not only have the religions built their impressive edifices, they have also developed their wonderful ceremonies, their calls to prayer, their bells, and their incenses.

Today many still profess to follow one of the main religions – Judaism,

Christianity, Buddhism, Hinduism and Islam – but there is a rising tide, especially in educated western societies, of those who cannot bring themselves to believe in a God who watches their every move, and judges every person, and has done so since time immemorial with a view to providing or denying everlasting life. Moreover, the written words that have been passed from each God to an appointed prophet and which are therefore the words of a perfect being and are inviolate, do not reflect the knowledge gained since they were first written, as they would if they were the words of an all-knowing and perfect being.

Many still follow a religion because they enjoy the impressive rituals of that religion – the calls to prayers, the incense, the magnificence of the regalia, the theatre and pageantry of the leaders of the prayers, the majesty or simplicity of the places of prayer – and they are attracted to the possibility of everlasting life in paradise. And there is the incredible bonus of feeling assured that they are special and one of a select group. So it is not surprising that there are now still many adherents to the religions and that there will continue to be adherents, but education is slowly whittling away at their numbers in educated societies.

Although there are many good reasons for doing away with the religions – the killings over the centuries and today in the cause of one or other of the religions, the encouragement of some religions for families to have many children in order to boost numbers in a world that is probably nearing capacity (See *"The Population Flood"*), the disdain, even hatred, of one religious order for another – there is a problem. What will replace the religious experience? How are we going to provide a meaning to life and the emotional fillips that religions give and that so many want?

The answer could lie in humankind developing, spreading and living by a new code, a code that lays down how we should live, and why we should live that way; a new set of clear and simple commandments. The creation of such a code of commandments should not be beyond the capabilities of a select group of scholars. It would certainly be superior to the ten that Moses brought down from the mount for Jews and Christians. It would also be superior to the murderous sections of the Qur'an with their calls for beheadings of infidels. Both are badly out of date.

The aim of the code would not be the worshipping of a divinity, but of giving humanity reasons for living peaceful and productive lives. It should not insist on the divine correctness of adhering to one approach to life and encouraging its followers to lop off the heads of non-followers as the Qur'an does, but it should lay down that its aim is to provide peace and to use the energy of humankind to look after those living on our limited globe, to advance our understanding of our limited world and its surrounds, to limit damaging violence and to advance science.

I believe that such a code is certainly possible and that if the great majority of humanity could be persuaded to live by its tenets our globe would be a better, safer and more liveable place, but I do not hold out much hope. I fear that deep-seated tribal instincts will prevail and that different racial, political and religious groups will continue to quarrel until violence erupts. We naked apes are not peaceful animals. I fear that there is no emotion driving us into uniting into one peaceful humanity, and that squabbling over perceived wrongs and inequities will supersede unity.

I believe that humankind has not yet developed to a stage in which it wants to, and can, live in peace and concentrate on universal welfare. The animal instincts of my tribe being superior to your tribe, my skin colour being superior to your skin colour, and my tribe's abilities being superior to your tribe's abilities, will continue, will prove to be too strong and will lead to more destruction. I fear that destruction will continue to occur, possibly to the point of extinction. I hope I am wrong.

# 8. SEXUALITY AND EQUALITY.

Language, both written and verbal, is the means we use to communicate with each other. To be able to communicate clearly requires that words have specific meanings that are generally understood. Today there are those who want to remove clarity from some words in the name of equality. They consider that words that make it clear what a person's sexual orientation is, or what the relationships between pairs of people are, lead to inequality. I disagree. The main driving force behind names given to people or their relationships should be clarity, not obfuscation for political correctness.

I am not sure when the nonsense of clouding gender issues began but I first noticed it when female thespians were no longer called actresses. For some reason that defeats me, both males and females have now to be called actors – except when it comes to awards. They are still given to actors and actresses. Calling all thespians actors only clouds whether they are a man or a woman, and I cannot see how that makes things either clearer or more equitable.

Now there has been a successful push to cloud the meaning of words that describe personal relationships with a huge fuss being made over the word 'marriage', a fuss that has cost millions of dollars for a plebiscite and that has involved a parliament that should have much more important issues to occupy it than the meaning of a word. My Concise Oxford English Dictionary says marriage is *"The formal union of a man and a woman, typically as recognised by law"*. Now that definition is being changed in the name of 'equality'.

For most of my life marriage has been a legal contract between a man and a woman, and I see no reason for changing that. Most understand the OED definition. Now a small and noisy group have made the word marriage apply to contracts between two males, two females or two people of other sexual proclivities, all in the name of equality. I consider this is not even vaguely reasonable. It is clouding the long term meaning of the word without achieving anything. Why should the meaning of a word be changed? I realise that a couple other than a male and a female want their union to be as important as marriage, and I agree that it should be, but I do not agree that they should take the word marriage and change its meaning.

Let me make it clear that I have no objection to people of any sexual persuasion living together and entering into binding contracts if that is their choice. What I cannot digest is that these people feel the need to call their liaison by the name of a union that does not apply to their union. Why do they wish to do that? Is it because they are attempting to hide the truth of their union from the world? If so why would they want to do that? Why would it not be better for all concerned for new and appropriate terms to be invented that applied to these different unions and that would show the world that these unions are permanent and legal? People with sexual preferences that are different to heterosexuals have no qualms about flaunting their personalities in gay pride marches, so why would they want to hide the truth of their living and loving arrangements from the world? Why do they want to pirate a term that disguises their lifestyle when they should be proudly advertising it?

Members of the human race are not uniform in stature, colour, intelligence, political or religious beliefs, or sexuality. These differences should not be the basis for discrimination as they have been in the past. They can be matters that are discussed but they have to be generally accepted because they exist. Just as a person should not be criticised for their size, their colour, political affiliations or religious beliefs (unless those beliefs are destructive as the beliefs of branches of the Muslim religion are) she or he should not be thought less of, or more of, because of inborn sexuality. In my view it is reasonable to have discussions on these topics, but they must not become emotional or heated and they should not become vituperative or lead to violence. A person's characteristics are as they are. They should not lead to that person being considered inferior.

Because I consider that a person's sexual orientation should not be a matter of judgement of the worth of a person, I have never understood why some religions have taken such negative stances to persons who do not conform to the majority male/female breakdown. It is, in my opinion, a reason why religions should be consigned to the rubbish bin of history.

Although I consider any negative discrimination against people because of their sexuality is wrong, I also believe that those with any sexual proclivity – heterosexual, homosexual, bisexual, transgender, you name it – have the responsibility not to try to force their choice on other humans, especially young humans, with the aim of leading others into their life style. People, especially young people, have the right to develop naturally without being led down any particular path by those wishing to exploit them, and a male/female led family is probably the best environment for that to occur. I also do not agree with the young being schooled in the various forms that sexuality can take. Left alone, the young will develop their own sexuality as all animals do. Teaching other possible forms of sexual activity than those to which they naturally aspire can only bring about confusion and, possibly, unfortunate experimentation. Only the wicked would want to change the young's natural and inborn sexuality.

Sexual activity has been designed by nature for the reproduction of animal species. Humans have modified it from that simple basis into a form of pleasure with, I understand, a number of different ways that pleasure can be enjoyed. It is probably because there has been a bias against sexual activity that does not involve the possibility of conception, especially in religions, that society has condemned those activities in the past. However it is now clear, in our world of an ever growing population, that it is time to slow population growth, so that those who follow their leanings to indulge in activities other than those that lead to reproduction are not acting in a damaging manner, unless they are harming their partner, so they should not be condemned or punished. It is even possible that the rise in the number of non-heterosexual people could be related to the overcrowding of our limited globe, and be one of nature's ways of slowing population growth and protecting our earth from destruction.

Returning to my original theme of sexuality and equality – as you can see I have no argument against any form of sexual activity by others, provided there is no physical violence to a partner and that it is not made compulsory. However I am against calling unions, other than the unions between heterosexuals, 'marriage' purely because the word was already taken by the man/woman union. If we are to have new legal unions, as I believe we should, we should find new names for them. Perhaps a competition could be held and the results judged by an LGBTI panel who could select names for the unions that they could broadcast with the same pride with which they now show their rainbow coloured flag. Live and let live.

## 9. HUMAN ARROGANCE.

We humans, we *Homo Sapiens*, the remaining one of the genus *Homo* not now extinct – a genus that included *Homo Erectus, Homo Habilis, Homo Ardipithecus, Homo Australopithecus* and *Homo Neanderthalensis* – have assumed that because we are currently at the top of our planet Earth's life forms, we are extremely important – but are we really? We consider that other forms of life are there so that we can demonstrate our superiority by exploiting them in many ways – by killing them to eat or for sport, by putting them to work for us, and by keeping them in positions of servitude as pets. Our dominance of the other species on our planet demonstrates that we reign supreme, but does it show that we are really important? Perhaps the answer is "No".

Our sense of self-importance manifests itself in several different ways, some of which are not pleasant. One of the manifestations of our self-importance is the religions that have been promoted by humans over the ages to provide answers to the questions of the position each of us occupies in relation to other humans and to eternity.

Most of the early religions had many deities and believed in either a life after death or reincarnation. Most had the belief that how a person was treated after death depended on how they had lived, but not all believed that. For instance, the Aztec religion believed that how you died determined your position in your afterlife. Later religions have generally believed in a supreme deity and an everlasting life for those worthy.

The Christian religion believes that humanity is made in the image of God, a supreme piece of self-importance. It means that God must come in several colours and shapes. Most of the leading religions have also invented an essence that only humans can have called, by speakers of English, a 'soul', which lives on eternally after the body expires. These unprovable beliefs – that humanity is made in the image of God, that each human possesses a soul, and that where our soul finishes up for eternity rests on how each person performs here on earth – have been bequeathed to us by a God that was not clever enough to spread the good word personally so It entrusted Its truths to sole human beings – Moses, Jesus Christ and Muhammad. This was a strange way in which to persuade the whole of the human race that there is an all-powerful God and of convincing humanity that it should behave according to a code of conduct to be granted everlasting life. Both the Qur'an and the New Testament, the books on which the two religions of Islam and Christianity are based, were written well after the deaths of Muhammad and Jesus, so both have shadows of doubt about them. Surely, an all-powerful deity would have arranged a better way for Its word to be spread to humanity than to have relied on a single entity who had little authority and did not commit his God's word to a lasting format but left that task to those who came years later, and worked from memory or oral history.

I realise that those devoted to the religion of their choice will disagree, but the very fact that the three monotheistic religions – Judaism, Christianity and Islam – are at loggerheads, and have been for centuries, is a strong indication that all are flawed and that none are the word of God. They are all the product of followers of people of doubtful balance, and they have been perpetuated by different tribes to show their superiority.

If, instead of believing there is an all-powerful deity who takes a detailed personal interest in each of us, that we have a 'soul', and that we will spend eternity in a blissful paradise if we behave well, we assume there is no personal deity, no essence that is a 'soul' and no everlasting life, the driving forces of our lives alter. We change from a God-like creature into being just another animal, albeit one who is intelligent enough to realise that for our future well-being on our limited globe we must learn to live within the globe's means, and that we have to live with others, and not consider them inferior because they are different. We then become both less important, but more responsible for our future.

Our history of wars between tribes and peoples, that is now often seen as heroic, and is celebrated in various ways, becomes silly, sad and juvenile squabbling having the sole beneficial virtue that, aided by these wars and (God given?) plagues of one sort and another, the numbers of humans on the planet have been kept down to manageable levels in the past. As we rely less on a mythical God, the existence of which is, at best, unproven, and as we become responsible for our own future, we must meet this responsibility, and instead of warring we must concentrate on living within the production capacity of our limited globe. We must stop any posturing and threatening and all work together, or we will destroy our only home, our Earth. God is not there to help us any more than She, He or It was there to save the dinosaurs.

Whilst this appears quite clear to me I have little real hope that the present 7.6 billion of us will join in working together to ensure our future. To meet the challenges in front of us requires rational thinking. For humanity to think rationally requires a widespread understanding of the situation, and that requires universal and balanced education.

Unfortunately there are many billions who do not have the opportunity for such a balanced education, who prefer to stay with their personal God who watches over them, or who prefer to continue to consider themselves superior despite evidence to the contrary. There will continue to be Christians who will believe in their own and only God, and Muslims who will believe that the teachings of their Qur'an, including its several calls for killing infidels when the opportunity arises, are God given, and there will always be those who will seek personal power and aggrandisement instead of working for the common good.

Then there is the deep seated animosity between tribes that is unlikely to disappear. For reasons that I do not understand those with different racial characteristics do not trust each other and often dislike each other. These differences can flair into violence, often started by megalomaniacal leaders with personal power as their driving force. If the world is to have a peaceful future these differences have to be put aside. That does not appear to be likely. It also appears that parts of the human race are as inclined to murderous conflict as ants in different colonies are, and that this enjoyment of battle will continue to manifest itself. Unless humanity wants peace and is prepared to cooperate to achieve it, a peaceful future is not possible.

There is also the incredible problem of the leaders humanity chooses. It has a history of following leaders who have combative natures and who do not hesitate to spill the blood of their followers. In the past there has been Alexander the Great, Julius Caesar, Genghis Khan and Tamerlane. More recently militant leaders have been Napoleon Bonaparte, Benito Mussolini, Adolph Hitler, Josef Stalin, Hideki Tojo and Douglas McArthur, and now we have Kim Jon-un, and we have even had warrior Presidents of the USA.

Based on the history of the past and the nature of personkind the chances of humanity working together to conquer the real problems of the world – nurturing and feeding the ever-increasing population, stemming pollution, providing useful work for humans in a world becoming more and more run by computers and robots, providing clean water and electric power, and other necessities and luxuries of life, providing universal and balanced education, and providing challenges other than conflicts – are slender to non-existent. To solve our problems will require humans to realise they are not as important as they now consider themselves to be, and that our Earth could watch humanity pass away as it once watched the great and powerful dinosaurs die out. Humanity is not God's supreme creation.

# 10. THE MOTIVATIONS OF HUMANS.

Throughout my life a major puzzle for me has been – what are the driving forces that govern the activities of people, and why do some appear to be good, some evil, some productive and some destructive? Why do we behave as we behave and do what we do?

I think I almost understand some of our basic motivations. We all start life with inbuilt drives for food, safety, shelter, warmth and freedom from danger. Then, as we mature, we can be driven by challenges of various types – both physical and mental – pride in achievement, companionship, sexual urges, and curiosity. We find we want to learn different things and to have different experiences. These urges are necessary for the survival and advancement of humanity and they appear to be good.

However there is a range of other motivating forces that do not appear to be helpful to us and I do not understand why we still have them. What positive purposes are served by physical aggression, destruction, jealousy, envy, hatred, avarice, superiority, anger, vanity, despair and an urge to dominate, in a civilised, society? How do these help in the continuing well-being of the human race? Do they still have a purpose or are they remnants from our animal ancestors – appendices with no further use but which can poison us? Should we be attempting to rid ourselves of these unpleasant and unhelpful traits?

Now I intend to discuss some of the drives that I do not understand and some I do.

Why do some of us pursue great wealth, and does that pursuit have harmful or advantageous consequences? Is wealth's pursuit because the individuals who devote their lives to pursuing wealth gain a feeling of superiority from appearing on the rich list? Is it only because of a natural greed? Or is it that by accumulating wealth they can be of benefit to society? Perhaps it is because the accumulation of wealth is a game that some are able to play better than others.

Is the accumulation of wealth in one pair of hands a good thing or a bad thing? Obviously that depends on what that pair of hands does with it. If the owner of the hands uses it to create real wealth by growing food, exploiting the buried riches in the earth's surface or making things that are useful, then I consider that having the wealth in that pair of hands is a good thing. Henry Ford developed mass production of his cars and raised the pay of his workers so they could afford his vehicles. Most would consider this a good thing but, given the plethora of vehicles today, I am not so sure.

However if the wealth has been accumulated only for the sake of accumulation – to satisfy an inbuilt greed – and it is being used as a base for further accumulation or as a base for wielding power and supporting a life of expensive ostentation, then I consider it is not admirable.

I note that the *Financial Review's* Australian Rich List consists mainly of investors, property developers, entertainers and sporting persons, financial service providers and retailers of goods, with the occasional mining magnate, agriculturist, manufacturer, and computer wizard thrown in. By far the preponderance of the wealthy have accumulated their wealth in pursuits that might accumulate wealth but are not from pursuits that actually produce wealth. Now I know that most of us want a lifestyle that is as comfortable as possible, but the drive of some to accumulate huge sums, to live in houses that are far bigger than they need to be and to live ostentatiously mystifies me. Perhaps it is an attempt to achieve immortality by leaving edifices with their names proudly displayed on them or, maybe, extreme wealth is a prop for weak personalities.

Why do some pursue political power in the present system? They will all say that they are driven by a wish to serve their community or their country, and if that is their motive it is admirable. But if they are driven by a wish for power and they actually enjoy the rough and tumble of the adversarial approach that is the current western world's political system, it is my belief that they are the wrong people to lead. It is also my opinion that the processes, by which candidates for parties are selected, are badly flawed, and that the selection processes and the menageries that are our parliaments do not attract those with the necessary experience – the thinkers and visionaries – who would lead to a better future. Even if experienced, thoughtful and balanced persons manage to find their way through the minefields of the selection processes and have successful election campaigns, and some do, they will not necessarily be successful parliamentarians because the successes are the communicators – union officials, teachers, journalists, lawyers – not the thinkers and doers.

The manner in which politics is now conducted in most western, democratic countries is not conducive to reasoned debate or to thoughtful answers to difficult questions. (Also see *"Democracy and Its Flaws"*).

Then there is the added problem for those who are selected, and who should be fully engaged in considering the complex problems of the country and finding successful solutions to them, that they have the expected duties of walking around shopping centres, smiling and shaking hands at kindergartens, attending ceremonies of one sort or another, making promises of benefits to groups from the public purse and opening public works. Often a parliamentarian's first concern is being re-elected, not guiding the country. These are not ideal working conditions for people who should be solving our country's difficult problems.

I believe all intending parliamentarians should be asked why they want the role and responsibility, and what particular skills and abilities they will bring to their roles other than their ability to debate and to charm, and the public should have that knowledge when it votes. They should also be tested for the workings of their consciences. (See *"The Necessity for a Conscience"*).

Having been part of the group that has the urge to build things I think I understand that group's motives. I am probably biased but I consider the design and construction of civilisation's buildings, transportation systems, dams, infrastructures, power producers and distributors, communications systems, manufacturing facilities, mines, machines, living and working accommodation, civic buildings, schools and universities, hospitals, sporting arenas and places of worship to be some of the greatest, if not the greatest, accomplishments of the human race.

I realise that the human race survived for many millennia without buildings by sheltering in caves, in igloos or in tents, but civilisation only came into being when the decisions were taken to cultivate and store food and to adopt, train and husband parts of the animal kingdom for transport, added power, food and clothing. It was these decisions that led to us being what we now are. They led to refinements in buildings and infrastructures and from there into humanity's searches for knowledge and scientific answers – quests that are ongoing. This is not to ignore or downplay the importance of the producers of our food.

The world of today owes much to Imhotep and his Step Pyramid at Saqqara. His Pharaoh, Djoser, made the mistake of uniting the separate states of Upper and Lower Egypt. Until they were united the Egyptians would plant their crops, and while they were growing and before they needed harvesting and storing, Upper and Lower Egypt would have a war. Once they were united something else had to be found to fill in the time for idle hands. Imhotep came up with the idea of building a burial plot, a mastaba, for his Pharaoh and the Step Pyramid came into being. He was the world's first project manager and his leadership led on to the Great Pyramids of Giza and later, the magnificent works of Rameses II and others.

Builders and designers find a great deal of satisfaction in producing their constructions for the use of their fellows. When humans are building they are being productive, and when they are productive, they are not destructive. They are peaceful and contented. Building is good for humanity. It is challenging and can bring out the best in those who are involved. We need more builders and less destroyers.

This brings me to the question of why, over many centuries, so many leaders have been bent on destruction. What motivates some people to destroy things, and why is destruction so often applauded? The western world feels justified in its destruction of Berlin, Nagasaki and Hiroshima in the Second World War, and I suppose the Germans felt justified in flattening large sections of London and other English cities. Today we look dispassionately at the destruction of Raqqa on our TV screens and mourn the destruction of ancient statues of Buddha by Moslems. Bombs are exploded in mosques.

What drives these terrible acts? Why did, and does, Kim Jong-un tweak the sensitive nose of Donald Trump? Surely he can not believe that he can take on the military and destructive might of the western world, and that he and his followers would survive, let alone triumph. Was it fear that led him to declare his high regard for Trump, or only diplomacy? Why do the North Koreans follow Kim? Surely they can see that he is not balanced.

But then, why did the energetic and organised Germans follow a bitter man and his cohorts who were still smarting from the defeat of an earlier war and who were unhappy with the financial successes of the Jewish section of their community? His energetic followers initially led Germany into becoming more prosperous and building an army but why, then, did they continue to follow the Fuehrer when he decided on invasion of the Sudetenland and later the whole of Europe?

Watch the incredibly well drilled armies of today's Fuehrer, Kim, goose stepping on the broad avenue of Pyongyang followed by huge weapons of destruction, and wonder how far the fat and unbalanced young man will lead his people into destruction and why they appear to willingly follow.

If you follow the history of destruction it appears that it is part of human nature. Is it? Is destruction and renewal part of a necessary cycle? Is it possible to change this destructive bent, or will we continue to develop and then destroy? Would a balanced education change things, as I believe it could, or are we too embedded in our cycle of development and destruction? Time will tell.

A question that besets me is – what motivates people to steal? Those who are acquisitive will only really enjoy the objects they desire if they earn them. As I have said elsewhere in these essays, ownership is the necessary basis of civilisation, for good or ill, so that those who steal are attacking the very foundations of the civilisation that supports them.

When people steal they must be motivated by two of the undesirable drivers of human nature – envy and avarice. Western societies pay lip service to stealing being wrong, but in a most half-hearted fashion. It is not portrayed as an attack on society, and forms of stealing from the public purse are often found to have been practiced by society's leaders.

Newspapers often have stories about persons in positions of authority, persons who should be leading by example, who abuse their positions by spending public money for personal benefit. Businesses manipulate their profits and export them to tax havens to avoid paying taxes. Union officials and businesses reach agreements that benefit both at the expense of workers. Companies that are supposed to be in competition come to agreements that enable them to take excessive profits from an unknowing public.

Why do these things take place? Why is stealing so widespread? Because the top end of society, the financially elite, is happy to cheat for profit and rewards itself so ridiculously lavishly, it leads the lower levels of society, the workers and producers, to feel free to exploit the economy by any means at their disposal. Corruption, both legal corruption and illegal corruption, becomes almost normal. It is a way of conducting our affairs that will destroy Australia's finances and will lead to another financial depression, if it is left unchecked.

How would it be possible for Australia to become a society free of corruption in which people expect to receive only what they have earned or what has been freely given to them? Why is stealing – taking from society more than has been earned or freely given – so widespread? Why is it that those who have accumulated a fortune by manipulation of finances to directly benefit themselves, or by directly stealing, are often applauded by the government and the public? Was Ned Kelly a nasty killer or a folk hero? Would society be better off if all attempted to earn more than they take, or is this utopian nonsense that is counter to human nature? Is humanity innately corrupt? From the manner in which so many of the successful conduct themselves it appears it is. Can ethics and good manners be taught to the young or is humanity destined to continue to steal and behave corruptly? Will humanity ever learn that it is better to build than to destroy and better to produce than to take? I hope so.

# 11. RIGHTS, RESPONSIBILITIES AND DEBTS.

Currently I read, and hear, a good deal about people's rights but not a lot about their responsibilities. Why is that? With the privileges of rights for all, the burdens of responsibilities for many surely follow. Or does the present population of Australia consider that rights and privileges do not have to be earned – that they are the gift of a deity? If they are not earned by someone, from where are they to come? As responsibilities are the counterbalances of rights, why are responsibilities not discussed as seriously and as often as rights, and what are really privileges – especially by the left and the Greens?

For a moral and civilised society to operate as successfully as possible in the present world requires all of its able persons to contribute as well as they can, and to expect only fair rewards for their inputs. Once people start claiming benefits from the government as their right, democracy is in trouble. Claims on the public purse are not rights, they are privileges, and accepting unearned benefits by anyone detracts from the health of both the society and the moral fibre of the claimant of the privileges.

Of course a moral society has an obligation to look after damaged persons, and does so. In my view even those persons damaged by accident, age, disease, mental impairment or other infirmity should, in return for being nurtured, attempt to contribute to their society as best they can, both for the health of their society, and because contributing will give a sense of accomplishment that helps provide the contributor with a sense of wellbeing. If a person is capable of trimming and weeding a garden (as little old ladies do in the beautifully kept public gardens of Japan), of making something for the needy, or of helping the badly damaged in some way, such as providing companionship, they should do those things. This all appears to be simple and reasonable to me but it does not appear to be readily understood by a big percentage of the population who seem to think it is better to take than to give – that to consume is better than to efficiently produce, and that just because they live in Australia they have entitlements.

According to a document sent to me by the Taxation Department, nearly 40% of my taxation dollar went to 'Welfare' last year. When welfare is added to the money spent on the aged, family benefits, the disabled and the unemployed 75% of my taxation was spent on these non-productive areas. Is this balanced spending by a sound and thoughtful government for a vital, healthy and thriving society, or is it an indication that candidates for parliament are attempting to buy votes?

Parliamentary parties now offer benefits to members of the non-contributing sectors of society, who have a say that is equal to that of members of the productive sector, as to who is given political leadership, in order to attract their votes. This is resulting in candidates who have high moral standards and want to build a better Australia, attracting a lower percentage of the available votes. Those who want to encourage all who can, to contribute, are not given the reins of power. Votes are, instead, given to those who make promises of hand-outs that have not been earned and really cannot be afforded.

This results in a major downside that is discussed little – if at all. Because both main Federal governing parties have provided high levels of largesse, Australia is now some $530 billion in debt, according to Cory Bernardi. Each of us – both Australian citizens who are productive and those who are not – owe over $22,000, and each of us has an interest bill of over $600 per year. Because only approximately one half of the population is employed, this means that the employed – both those permanently employed and those only employed part time – owe over $44,000 and, each year, are responsible for over $1,200 in interest on the money owed by the Commonwealth. When this is added to the $56 billion owed by the Western Australian government our total debt per person in WA is about $43,000, our debt per worker is approximately $85,000 and our total interest bill is some $2,500 per year for each worker. Surely this is ridiculous, economic profligacy by our leaders – those who control these things – since the Rudd, Gillard, Turnbull and Barnett governments went on their spending sprees.

All thinking Australians, should be ashamed that Australia is in such a poor financial position. And the general electorate who put these people in power should also be ashamed. No sensible family or reasonably and logically run business would operate in such a way. The excuse that is trotted out is that we are not as badly off as several other countries. We may have fallen off the edge of the financial cliff, but we are not falling as fast as others. Why has this been allowed to happen and is it possible to do something about it? Only a concerted effort by the bulk of our population will stop the rot.

As I wrote earlier, a moral society has an obligation to nurture damaged people but that obligation should be accompanied by the obligation of all citizens who are able to do so, to willingly carry out tasks, and to carry them out as well as they can. Those who can be productive, in any way, should be productive. I know this flies in the face of the fact that there is a shortage of full time work in Australia but the reasons for this shortage need to be found and removed. Is it because workers in Australia expect – in fact demand through their unions – a good deal more for their labour than their counterparts in other countries and/or are they less productive? The world is now a universal market place so that if we are to compete in that market we will have to compete on an equal footing whether we like it or not. We need to either produce more efficiently – as we do with our mining, agriculture and several of our professions – or we need to expect less. Australians cannot expect to continue to get more than their opposite numbers in a global market. And this rule also applies not only to unionists, those with manual skills and labourers, but also to incredibly overpaid CEOs and high level civil servants.

An unfortunate side effect of our democratic system is that to get elected candidates must pander to minority groups. They have been known to offer our funds for projects that lack economic feasibility and unsupportable life cycle costs, but that appeal to sections of the community. Examples are royalties for regions (nobody wants to meet the costs of running several of the buildings that were built or to pay for maintaining them), paid maternity and paternity leave (how did my young wife and I have and maintain six children without it?) and passive Aboriginal welfare (despite the fact that the Aboriginal lawyer and wise man Noel Pearson is opposed to it). Many have taken financial benefits from the government to the detriment of us taxpayers. These schemes appear to me to be efforts to buy votes but they are unlikely to stop until the majority of the electorate condemns the practice.

Now a large, and often reasonably wealthy, section of the community competes to gain a share of the public purse on the grounds that they have paid tax for many years and are entitled to their share. As Oliver Wendell Holmes is reported to have said – taxation is the price of civilisation – so they have already enjoyed the benefit of their taxation dollar in the roads and services that have been built, in the schools and university buildings which their children attend, the very expensive hospitals that deal with their ailments, in the defence of our country, and in transport systems that operate at a loss. This acceptance by many, that taking from the country's economy is a reasonable thing to do, is not the attitude my father's family had and it is not mine. I realise that I am fortunate to work at a profession in which I could still be active at the age of 85, that I was privileged to be asked to provide advice in structural engineering matters, and I even considered myself privileged to still be paying tax, even though I was, and am, far from happy with what was, and is, being done with much of it. Now, at 86, I am retiring because both my energy levels and my ability to solve problems are deteriorating.

I regret that the independent spirit that drove much of the Australian population when I was young, a spirit that built the Australia we now see around us, appears to have largely evaporated and has been replaced by the bulk of the population anxiously scrabbling for themselves with the honourable now in the minority. Or is that just sad and cynical thinking by an out of phase, aging grey head?

# 12. DECEITS.

Deceit, the act of providing false information in order to make a gain of some description, is a widely practised art. Why are deceits so popular in Australia and the nations of the world generally? Where are they leading us?

There are, of course many levels of deceit from the extremely personal to those that affect nations. Some are aimed at providing a nation with an advantage. Some are aimed at providing financial or other benefits to the deceiver. Some can be aimed at protecting others from a destructive truth. Some are the productions of distorted imaginations or hysteria – the result of mental disturbances – and can be quite innocent or quite destructive. Deceit can be viciously untruthful or it can be relatively benign. This is all clear, but why is deceit now so widespread, and why does it appear to becoming more and more mainstream? Why is truth not more respected, and practised? Even when deceit is aimed at protecting someone, is that really beneficial or would it be better if truth prevailed?

It is my view that we all live in a world of myths and fabrications – of deceits – and we happily accept and perpetuate many of them. A prime example of a popular deceit – one that is still a powerful deceit that has affected the human race detrimentally – and in my view is humanity's main deceit – is that all-powerful deities entrusted Their truths and Their divine messages to single individuals and not to the population of the whole world which, being all powerful, They could have easily done.

There are other, less potent, deceits such as that America, Russia and China are nations bent on peace, not nations bent on domination, and that Santa Claus delivers presents on Christmas Eve. The deceit, by which many live, that by living to the tenets of a religion, even one that calls for striking the heads off infidels, everlasting life in paradise will be granted, is a deceit that needs to be put into the basket of history. There is also the incredible and self-serving belief that humanity, in its many guises, colours, shapes and sizes has been modelled by the deity on His, Her or Its image, making humanity a uniquely special group on this, our one and only Earth.

Unfortunately it is not possible for all three of the monotheistic religions with their beliefs in the divinity of their own religion to all be followers of the one true God, comforting as that belief is. My conclusion is that religions of all kinds, from the many Gods of India, to the ancient Gods of Egypt, Greece and Rome, to the breakdown of the Christian religion at the time of the Reformation, and to the split of the Moslem religion into its two main sects, are human inventions and are, therefore, deceits.

Despite the fact that all monotheistic religions, including Judaism, considers they have direct contact with an all-powerful deity, all have had huge problems throughout their histories, and continue to have problems to this day. All have experienced attacks, mass killings, ill treatment and other inter-tribal nastinesses. Based on their records it is not possible to come to any conclusion but that religions are deceits brought to life by the overheated imaginations of unbalanced people. This is unlikely to be a widely accepted view, but I defy anyone to produce a better balanced explanation for their histories. Not one of the monotheistic religions can possibly be the truth. (For additional confirmation as to the deceits of the Christian religion see the writings of Richard Dawkins).

Humanity has always dreamed of life after death, People have never wanted to accept that they are accidents of evolution with no more right to eternity than slugs or fleas, that their existence is limited to their short life span on our limited globe, and that they have no alternative but to make the best they can of their limited time alive. It is this wish for eternity that has made the deceit of religion the most powerful deceit of humanity. It has been used to control the masses since the time of the Pharaohs and the Aztecs.

There are, of course, many deceits other than religions, but it is religions that are all pervading, and are the base of many of the world's tribal problems. It is religious differences that have led to the current deadly frictions in the Middle East, that have resulted in Israel arming itself and, sometimes, behaving aggressively to protect itself.

Religious differences have brought down airliners and crashed other aeroplanes into iconic buildings killing thousands. Religions have the ability to raise passions to a pitch at which killing is regarded as justifiable, by those who believe in a militant God that no-one has ever seen. It is possible that it is not really religion that causes sections of humanity into carrying out stupid and nasty attacks on other sections of humanity but that it has been twisted to satisfy those parts of society who are driven by base tribal instincts that find satisfaction in destroying other parts of humanity, and the results of their labours. If this is so, that it is not religion that causes parts of humanity to destroy other parts of humanity, but more deep seated tribal instincts, doing away with the deceits of religion is not likely to improve the behaviour of the warlike sections of the human population.

As I have said elsewhere in these essays, the real hope for world peace is broad and balanced education, but that will only be successful if people want to be educated and will reject their silly, destructive tribal instincts.

From what I regard as the worst of humanities deceits, religions, with their message that they are the saviours of personkind despite their bloody histories, I now descend to everyday deceits that are practised almost universally.

Some of the more egregious are covering up sexual crimes against people, especially young people. The Christian religion has a well-known track record in this area. Then there are the crimes of corruption, and the making of false statements, by those standing for office. These are now so common that they are expected. There are those who use their political position to gain huge financial benefits, as Mr. Eddie Obeid has been reported to have done.

Union officials disrupt trade and legitimate businesses, to show their power while, at the same time, taking from union slush funds for their personal use. Business leaders spend their energies limiting the tax their businesses have to pay whilst pocketing huge salaries for their efforts.

Australia appears to be awash with persons who deceive. Why? Why do deceivers feel entitled to practise their deceits? Why are they driven by a greed for profits and for personal wealth and not driven by a wish to contribute to society? Does the highly paid layer of society, that is the management layer, not realise that by rewarding themselves so lavishly they are encouraging the productive layer to demand more for less input and setting a business tone that will reflect badly on the competitiveness of Australian businesses? The leaders do not appear to be leading by example.

I now return to my original question of why deceit is so commonly practised. Based on the evidence available it appears that a large proportion of all levels of Australian society prefer to deceive to gain short term advantages than to subscribe to truth for long term improvement. Working harder for the future is left to the workers of China and South Korea. Deceit cannot lead to long term improvement of our country. Surely truth and honest effort are to be preferred. Why are they not universal in our country?

# 13. HONOUR/SUCCESS.

In my more pessimistic periods I see a bleak future ahead for our western, capitalistic, democratic society, unless there are changes from its present, frequent displays of rampant greed and/or lust for power by some of its leaders – both leaders in the political sphere and leaders of major corporations – and of its larger banks. We need changes in political and business morality. Then there are the attacks by imported religious zealots on innocent citizens, the billions spent arming for war (submarines and fighter planes for 'defence'), the obvious corruption in some of our religious organisations and our mindless idolising of actors and sports stars. A sad characteristic is that our western societies now appear to expect benefits from the public purse, and to be provided a higher standard of living than comparable societies elsewhere on our limited globe, without earning it. We are in severe debt, but that is hardly discussed.

   Contributing to society and behaving honourably were taught to me as the proper ways to behave in my impressionable youth. This now appears to be passé. I did not always follow what I was taught but, as you can read, I have not forgotten the lessons. Whilst we still admire and accolade those who serve, our greatest admirations are saved for those who win at games, who succeed in business, even if they bend the rules, and those who star in our many entertainments.

Does this mean, as I think it does, that western society is in a period of satisfying its immediate, shallow demands, not a period of service to the present, and more importantly, the future, generations? Is western society heading further into a period of decadence, as past great civilisations have done? Is it weakening and falling into a condition where it will be overrun by more dynamic and energetic societies? Is that already in the process of happening?

An early poem I learnt, that has stayed with me, is Sir Henry Newboldt's Vitai Lampada with its call to *"Play up! Play up! And play the game!"* Perhaps foolishly, I still believe its message, even if I have not always followed it in my lifetime.

About 2400 years ago Socrates was reported to have said *"The children now have luxury; they have bad manners, contempt for authority; they show disrespect for elders and love chatter in place of exercise. Children are now tyrants, not servants of their households. They no longer rise when their elders enter the room"*. Does this sound familiar? Is it a sign that children are always disrespectful or are there cycles during which children are not taught respect, followed by periods during which they are taught respect for their society, and the elders who have built that society, and who lead it? If there are cycles of respect/disrespect what brings about those cycles? To achieve general respect should a society be teaching it? Will a society that does not call for respect between all citizens achieve it?

There are many other questions that are related to the teaching of honour and respect that trouble me. A few of them follow.

- Can honourable behaviour be taught? Is it possible to teach manners, and respect for other people? If it is possible, why is teaching the young to be honourable in dealing with others in their society not part of early education? Given that Imams can successfully teach young Moslems to kill for Allah, and that it has been reported that the Catholic Jesuits' boast is that if they have the boy until he is seven they will give you the man, it should be possible to teach honour. If it is not possible to teach decency, honour and respect what hope is there for humanity?

- Are members of the human race generally honest and honourable by nature or are they conniving and self-serving? Are the primary motivations of many business and political leaders, especially those who are successful in both western capitalistic societies, and in the burgeoning societies of Russia and China, self-importantly wielding power and/or accumulating great wealth?
- Do the individuals who take more from their society than their due, realise that they are undermining that society because civilisation is based on ownership. Why do so many try to accumulate great wealth at the expense of those who actually produce it?
- Are those who seek power the right people to control it? The seekers after power in history have, almost universally, shown that they are not necessarily those who will lead to peaceful development. Consider Alexander the Great, the 4th century conqueror of much of the known world through bloody battles; Attila the Hun, the 5th century 'Scourge of God' who sacked and pillaged Roman cities; Tamerlane, the 14th century Islamist who looted parts of India and massacred thousands; Genghis Khan, who conquered most of Eurasia in the 12th century; Napoleon Bonaparte who led his French troops to many victories in the late 18th century and who was finally defeated at Waterloo in 1815 and exiled; Adolph Hitler, the Austrian who led Germany to a final defeat in the second World War and; Joseph Stalin the leader of communist Russia whose troops played a huge role in Germany's defeat. All of these have sought and gained personal power and have used it to conquer and kill many. Surely now the globe does not want, or need, militant leaders. What we now need are thoughtful and peaceful leaders to plan for a sustainable future. We do not need further conflicts but, looking at Putin, Kim Jon-un, Donald Trump, and many of the lesser leaders, it certainly appears that conflict is likely.
- Is the human race doomed to cycles of peaceful development followed by periods of destruction as armed forces, led by latter day Genghis Khans, slaughter each other, and destroy the creations of the peaceful and productive periods, as has happened so often in the past? Or has

humanity at last reached a stage where it realises that from further armed conflict there will be no winners – only poisonous destruction?

- Can humanity, which now has access to powerful, nuclear weapons with their long lasting destructive effects, afford to repeat the stupidities of the past? When the most powerful weapons were the guns and torpedoes of ships and submarines, long range cannons, aircraft laden with bombs and personnel carrying guns and rockets, their destructive powers were limited and the damage could be replaced, as the world saw as the destruction of World War 2 was replaced. Now the weapons of war are so powerful and the poisons they release are so long lasting they will leave devastated areas that cannot be readily replaced or renewed.

In my view what this all means is that for humanity to have a peaceful and productive future it needs honourable, balanced, intelligent and thoughtful leaders who have honest ambitions for a safe and stable Earth, and are not chasing personal power, aggrandisement or wealth, as so many leaders of the past appear to have done.

Is it possible to teach being honourable – the putting of others before yourself and aiming for the betterment of humanity, not personal position – or is it innate in some and completely foreign to others? Can education produce students whose main aim is to serve their society, or is it not possible to teach morality and conscience? Even if we believe that morality and honour cannot be taught, I do not consider that we have any option but to try to teach them, because it is humanity's only chance for a peaceful and prosperous future.

In the past, and even at present, societies and its leaders have persuaded the young to go into battle and to give up their lives for their country. Surely it should not be impossible to persuade the young and energetic to forego wealth and personal position to save the world of which they, and their descendants, are a part. Today religions are educating many of their young into believing there is a life after death, if they follow the tenets of their religion – which includes the killing of infidels. Why should it be more difficult to educate the young to believe that they need to behave honourably to achieve a successful and peaceful Earth?

# SECTION 2

# POLITICAL ISSUES

Are the western world's democratic systems as they are now practised ideal? Do they have flaws? If they do are improvements possible? Is our taxation system, based as it is on production, the best system? Is being politically correct necessary, and is it growing or fading as an imperative? How important is the giving and taking of offense? I think these matters need informed discussion.

## 14. DEMOCRACY AND ITS FLAWS.

As we all know, democracy is widely practised throughout the western world and those who practise it consider it the best, indeed the only reasonable, system for selecting our governments. But is it without fault? Is it serving future Australia as well as it should? Can the present system be improved?

In 1947 it was Winston Churchill who wrote *"Democracy is the worst form of government except for all those other forms that have been tried from time to time"* and that is almost certainly true – but is democracy, as it is now practised in Australia, without flaws, does it always produce the best balance of answers for a functioning society, is it possible to make improvements to the systems now practised, and do we in Australia, the electors, support it as we should?

Do we elect those who are driven by an ambition to serve their society, who will govern us with fairness and intelligence and with our long-term welfare as their prime aim, or do we elect those who present themselves well to the party they hope to represent, who aim for the importance, power and long term financial security a parliamentary position provides, and who offer us promises for an easier life?

Are we, the electorate, knowledgeable enough and clever enough to be able to discern the candidates who are able, fair and dedicated, from those who are glib and power hungry? Do we vote for those who promise a hard but fair road forward, or do we vote for those who promise us an easier path for the present but with a doubtful future? Are we swayed by emotional calls and do we – the entire electorate – study the pros and cons of issues such as climate change, 'free' education and medical treatment, family benefits and other government hand-outs in sufficient depth to make rational decisions?

Do those who stand – who have been selected by a party because they have agreed to toe the party line – have the talent and experience to make the correct decisions? Or are their drives wishes for prominence and power? Is it necessary that those who stand need to have a pleasant public persona, and be able to charm those with whom they come into contact, or should the electorate be more swayed by knowledgeable and dedicated persons, even shy persons, who have intelligence, learning and a deep understanding of society's problems and possibilities? To get elected do candidates need to espouse policies that are destructive in the long term to gain support from a voting public that can have as its main aim gratification of its more immediate desires, or can they stand on policies aimed at the long term welfare of those they represent? Is the western democratic system based, as it is, on warring parties – Liberal, Labor, Conservative, Republican, Democratic, Social, Green, Christian, National – the ideal approach to democracy, or should electorates be voting for people of ability and character, rather than people who follow a party line? And finally – does democracy as practised in Australia truly represent the wishes of the majority of Australians, or does our system have flaws?

Democracy in Australia has one obvious flaw. Those who have voted for other than the elected government must, nonetheless, live under that government and operate under policies with which they disagree. Provided the system is fair, and I will discuss this further, most of us in Australia would accept this flaw with equanimity, knowing that there will be another election in the near future.

However it can be, and has shown itself to be, a source of conflict in countries where militant minorities consider they are not being treated as they should be. It has led to armed insurrections. A thoughtful democracy must always consider its minorities but it must not pander to those minorities, as the Australian democracy often does, to satisfy some emotional need or feeling of guilt, or to garner a fringe vote.

Another defect I believe our present democratic system has is the silly, and often fake, nastiness of the parliaments themselves. The adversarial system, on which our law courts are based, has become the system our parliaments employ, possibly due to the large number of lawyers involved. Egged on by a press gallery only too anxious for noisy controversy, politicians spend time attacking each other instead of discussing the advantages and disadvantages of important issues and decisions.

A corollary to this juvenile state of affairs is that important matters that affect the welfare of all Australians can be pushed to one side as emotional issues that affect few, are shrilly debated and shrilly reported – gay rights, misogyny, offense, same sex marriage, climate change (when Australia emits only about 1.3% of the world's $CO_2$, and has no power to alter what is happening in other countries that produce much more of the gas), and apologies for events that occurred two hundred years ago and were certainly not of the present generation's making.

Our parliaments should not be crying over spilt milk but charting a way forward to a better future. They should be encouraging us to expect less and to perform better, and they should be aiming at an environment in which most will want to contribute to the future welfare of all, and not take as much from the efforts of others as they can. Voters are now encouraged to consider that the government is a bottomless pit of wealth, and each is entitled to a share, instead of realizing that the government can only spend what it receives (or that is all it should spend). Pride was once felt by those who knew they were contributing. Now the reigning drive appears to be to get as much as can be taken from the state. It is unhealthy and it will not last.

Parliament should be a place of measured discussion and thoughtful debate, not a place of almost childish wrangling. Discussion should centre on the important issues of Australia's place in the world – its political place, its financial place, its moral place and its contribution to the welfare of the world – and answers arrived at. Differences should be politely aired, backed by facts – not by emotional or snide outbursts – and resolved.

As it works in Australia democracy also has the flaw that many of those who are selected to stand, by a political party, are not necessarily thinkers, doers or those who are actively creative, and who have the necessary experience in the hurly burly of everyday commercial life. They are debaters and communicators, preferably with attractive personalities– lawyers, young activists with little experience who have grown up with, and have come through the ranks of a party, teachers, union officials, popular entertainers and sports people – people able to charm and exchange views with strangers. Those chosen are not normally diffident. They can be particularly successful if they have charisma, have a surety about their own opinions and are able to mix with crowds without feeling intimidated; indeed they must enjoy the cut and thrust of public discourse.

Are people with these attributes necessarily the best people to decide a society's direction? To be a politician in the present system requires that a person desires public exposure and wants to be in a position of public authority. People who want notoriety and authority are not necessarily those who should have the responsibility and authority of leadership. The leaders a society needs are those who have shown that they have the temperament, the intelligence, the necessary experience of the world and business, the learning, the understanding, the abilities, the balanced conscience and the staying power to lead. They must be able and prepared to shoulder the responsibilities that go with authority. They should not be those dazzled by the limelight of a high position.

This does not mean that all those who aspire to leadership roles are not qualified for those roles but it probably means that many with qualities that would make them ideal leaders are overlooked. Those who possess a likeable nature on television are not necessarily leadership material whereas sober individuals, individuals who are thoughtful and retiring but who are not personable, are likely to be better politicians, are likely to make better decisions, and be more successful leaders.

The systems that have developed throughout countries that practise democracy have become systems of expensive electioneering showmanship and personality. Democracy's leaders, who should be devoted to guiding the country – surely a full time task – instead, spend time point scoring in television debates, travelling around in specially decorated and expensive forms of transport, shaking hands and smiling. The lead up to the 2016 Presidential election in the United States was an incredible spectacle – but was it the epitome of democracy as it should have been? Were the two candidates who fought it out the best that America could provide? Were Hillary and Donald really ideal leadership material of the most powerful nation in this world, troubled as the world is by egomaniacal leaders such as Mugabe and Kim, or has the showmanship and cost of American presidential campaigns outrun the requirement of solidity and honesty, of intelligence and character? Would Harry S. Truman, Ronald Reagan or Dwight Eisenhower, all honourable and able presidents, stand a chance in today's show biz, political maelstrom?

The present processes by which democracy's leaders are selected are certainly flawed in my view. Most voters appear to be basing their choices on television interviews between candidates and professional interviewers often with their own agendas, advertisements that paint glowing pictures or attempt to denigrate, and articles produced by reporters with their own biases. Votes are cast without voters really knowing the candidates or really understanding what the candidate's motives or abilities are. The fact that so many politicians, of all political persuasions, are found, after they are elected, to be morally wanting, self-serving, and often self-enriching, or prepared to take personal benefits from the public purse, is a clear indication that the selection process has flaws. Better processes should be sought and different systems of candidate selection considered. Democracies need honourable and able leaders, not personable communicators and party apparatchiks.

Then there is the matter of the fairness of our electoral system. It is clear that it is theoretically possible for a party that gains a small margin of more than 25% of the total vote can get elected. To be successful all a party needs is to win the seats in 51% of the electorates and it only needs to win those with 51% of the vote in those electorates. If one party gains 51% of the electorates that are evenly balanced it will win, whereas if in 49% of the remaining electorates another party is overwhelmingly preferred, that party will still lose. The party that wins will have been elected by a minority of the voters.

Note that Donald Trump did not win the popular vote.

Is this a fair system? Obviously elections do not operate in such a marginal way in real life, but the system can certainly be and is, unbalanced and in some electorates a few, not committed to a major political group, can decide the successful candidate. Is it reasonable that a disenchanted fringe, or a fringe seeking personal gain, should be able to decide who governs and who is able to block legislation because it does not fit with that minority's platform?

The present democratic system in Australia has another flaw that, in my view, surpasses all others. It is never discussed. It is that there are forces at work that encourage voters to cast their votes for candidates who promise them immediate advantages. Although I do not wish to change the value of each individual's vote, there is a fundamental flaw in a system that gives a say to those who consume more than they produce that is equal to the say it gives to those who produce more than they consume. Once consumers become the group with the greater numbers – and that group votes for their immediate personal advantage – democracy is in trouble. When those who vote for benefits from their society's public purse outnumber those who wish to build for the future, to leave their society better than it was when they entered it, for future generations, and who strive to make that happen, democracy is a threatened system and financial collapse becomes inevitable. When the emphasis is on dividing the spoils rather than on producing the goods, when it is on entertainment not on production, and when the political parties are forced to pander to satisfying shallow demands to get elected, instead of leading to produce future wellbeing, a democracy is failing.

The only possible solution to the probability of a slow decline in our country's financial position is that the majority of Australians vote for, and work for, the general and long term welfare of their society, not for their own personal and immediate financial gain. Is this likely in today's Australia? Will voters, especially those who currently gain financial benefits from the public purse, today vote for a candidate who has *"nothing to offer but blood, toil, tears and sweat"*, as the United Kingdom did for Churchill in 1940, or even for a candidate seeking a reduction in the benefits many electors might be receiving, even if those benefits cannot be afforded? Today, with welfare consuming over one third of the total budget and with health consuming another one sixth, so that over half the total government expenditure goes into these non-productive areas, would any candidate be foolhardy enough reduce the amount being given to those voters, both the receivers of the benefits and those who control the benefits and are paid to tend the beneficiaries when, it appears, over fifty percent of the voting public could lose some income?

We need honourable and upright politicians with insight, work and business experience, courage, intelligence and understanding. They must stand on honest platforms devoid of false and unsustainable promises. The electorate must then select its leaders on the basis of the best long-term interests of our society. What we do not need are politicians who pander to the satisfying of immediate greed in slogans prepared by clever spin doctors, and broadcast by expensive advertising campaigns. And we certainly do not need voters to vote themselves benefits from the public purse. Is it likely that our society will vote for a sustainable future or will it continue to vote itself benefits until the debt becomes unsustainable and there is a crash?

For future prosperity we Australians need to produce more than we consume. We need to realise that we are in competition with the rest of the world and that we cannot expect to get a great deal more for our labour and our produce than others can for theirs. We cannot rely on temporary bonanzas such as the wool boom, the gold rush, the discovery of natural gas and the iron ore boom. Remember the faded Poseidon nickel boom and its aftermath. We must efficiently produce those things that we are able to produce, and we must produce them from businesses and corporations that are in Australian hands and that meet their Australian taxation responsibilities.

Australia is spending more than it is earning, and despite promises from all sides of politics that there will be a return to surplus sometime in the future (remember Wayne Swan, the world's greatest treasurer? He made such a promise. Now Mr. Morrison makes a similar promise). A surplus will not be achieved until production exceeds consumption. If it continues to spend more than it earns Australia will go deeper into debt until, finally, a halt will be called by the lenders and there will be a loss of living standards, as happened in the Great Depression. We are already selling assets to maintain our current living standards and once these are sold we will become a mendicant society that is largely owned by others. I do not believe that this is the future that most Australians want.

Is there a better democratic system than the system that we in Australia practice? Perhaps we should study the Swiss system, in which the voting public have a much more direct say in their federal constitution. In Switzerland the path into power is much closer to those voting for their representatives, and the term of federal leadership is limited to one year. It is not a platform for life. It certainly would not lead to a past prime minister finding herself or himself the proud possessor of $50 million as ex-Prime Minister Hawke was recently reported to have. How was this accumulated on a minister's salary?

We need the most honourable and experienced people in our parliament leading us, not those selected by a party for their loyalty to that party, and we should consider a system that will attract those people into parliament. Whatever system we decide to use our democracy must perform so that it is clear that it, with its several faults, not only works – it is the superior system.

# 15. THE POLITICAL SYSTEM.

For a society to be peaceful and prosperous it must have a political system that the citizens trust and hold in high regard. Is this the situation in Western democracies at this time?

Of the many leadership systems that have been tried by nations throughout history – Pharaohs thought to be immortal and God-like, emperors spreading their empires by force, national socialism led by a Fuehrer, hereditary monarchies, warrior leaders, communism – with all its faults the best so far produced by humanity appears to be democracy. (See *"Democracy and Its Flaws"*).

As it is now practised democracy certainly has flaws. It is supposed to be a system in which all citizens have a say. However in almost all western societies, in which it is the governing system, that say has been reduced to voting for, or perhaps more often, voting against candidates that have been chosen by an elite few in a political party, not by the electors. This can lead to 'branch stacking' and the selection of candidates who are amenable to the party's line, which might not be in the best long term interests of the majority of the population.

Most of those voting have little real understanding of the positions candidates will take, or of their courage, knowledge, experience and intellect, so they do not vote for or against a candidate but for, or against, a platform put forward by a candidate's party in an expensive advertising campaign that makes promises that, it is hoped, will appeal to the majority of the voters. There is no doubt that the system has produced some extremely poor leaders, some corrupt candidates who have nonetheless been successfully elected, and a good few self-servers. It has also produced many honourable people but they can be muzzled by 'party loyalty'.

It is my view that it is now time for Australia to re-visit its constitutional make-up to see if it is possible to improve on the existing democratic model. A review of the Swiss system, a system that appears to have produced a stable and prosperous country despite having almost no natural resources except Alps, and that appears to operate with quiet efficiency, could be a starting point. The Westminster System, with its adversarial approach to government, quite clearly has some operational flaws, and the American system with all its ridiculously expensive hoop-la has produced some incredibly mediocre leaders, and has now, as I write this, elected what could be a poor choice of President from a pair of candidates that I consider not to be the cream of the American polity.

Why not a review of alternative systems by those interested in Australia's future? I am a person who does not believe in fixing things that are not broken but I consider the Westminster System as it now operates is badly flawed. Does the majority agree with me?

We need the most honourable and experienced people in our parliament leading us, not those selected for their loyalty to a particular party or a particular mode of governing. We should consider a system that will attract the best of Australia's population into parliament to serve for a limited period. Whatever system is chosen our democracy must perform so that we can agree that it is a superior system.

## 16. AUSTRALIAN PARLIAMENTS.

Are Australia's many parliaments operating as they should? Are they serving Australia properly? Is how they conduct themselves, and are the issues they spend their time wrangling over, shining examples of democracy at its best? Is the adversarial approach taken by the various factions of which the parliaments are composed, the way in which our country's leaders should operate and cooperate? I do not think so.

Parliaments should be places of measured and thoughtful discussion by intelligent, thoughtful, experienced and balanced people about the important issues that affect our country. Are they? Or are they venues for wrangling between the left, the right, the greens, the nationalists and the minority groups, each with its own limited agenda? Are they venues for displays of self-importance, not displays of considered leadership?

They should be places of thoughtful debate – not places of ridiculous wrangling. The important issues of Australia's place in the world – its financial place, its political place, its defence place, its philosophical place as to the future and its moral place – and how it can contribute to the general welfare of our world, should be discussed and answers arrived at. Parliaments should be free of corruption and self-seeking. Differences should be aired politely and they should be backed by facts, not emotions. To be a member of parliament should be a duty undertaken by concerned and able citizens for a limited period. It should be a period of service to the nation, not a platform on which the self-important parade and show how adept they are at cutting down others with differing opinions. And it should certainly not be a platform for enriching its members, as it now appears to be.

For a parliament to be worthwhile, it should be run on the basis of mutual respect, and cooperation, with healthy disagreements settled by intelligent and mature discussion. Parliaments should concentrate on issues that are important for the future of the country – issues of affordability of its decisions, how to better the country's health and education, its law and order, its position in the world, and with which other world powers it should best align and how, its immigration policy and, very importantly, how we can compete on the world market, and if we cannot, why we cannot.

Parliaments should be composed of people experienced in production of all types, in health and education, in legal issues, in finance, in the building and maintaining of infrastructure, in food production and preparation, and in managing businesses. It should not be composed of party apparatchiks with experience only of the cloistered world of politics, and little experience of the world of growing, mining, manufacturing or infrastructure – the real producers of our country's wealth – or with commerce, legal issues, education and health. Also, it should not be the sheltered home of many of those with vested interests, such as union officials, sports stars or entertainers (unless the representatives of each have other necessary qualifications) or those whose businesses rely heavily on government contracts.

All intending members of parliament should be subjected to a check as to whether or not they have a conscience, and only those with a conscience, and a clear objective to serve Australia, should be selected to stand. Those with the aim of self-importance, and who are likely to use their position for personal advancement, should not be allowed to serve.

I repeat – to be a member of parliament should be a duty that is taken on by concerned and able citizens for a limited period. It should be a period of service, not a platform for showing the world how important a person is, or for using public money to enrich a candidate, or to further a reputation. I find it fascinating that all leading ex-parliamentarians, despite the fact that they are not that well paid during their periods of service, appear to be able to live lives of expensive luxury after retirement.

An example is ex-prime minister Hawke. He rose from union official to lead the Labor party – neither position really well paid. He is now reported to be worth $50 million. Where did that come from? There are several others who appear to be wealthier than their remunerations would suggest they would be.

Parliaments should be forums that set the tone for behaviour for Australia's citizens. They should arrive at answers on the grounds of well-argued logic, not be the scene of sniping and personal attacks, of displays of animosity and inane one-up-man-ship. Parliament should not be a place for attempts at bullying, or for giving or taking offence.

Is this how Australia's parliaments conduct themselves or do they, often egged on by a media anxious for a news story that will titillate and shock, behave in an adversarial manner and spend time squabbling instead of carrying out logical discussions on matters of import?

I have criticised our parliaments, but is the truth that, not only do they appear to be often made up, in part, of people whose main drive is to get their hands on power, even if they are not really fit, in many cases, to use it, but that they reflect the quality of those who selected them to stand, and those who elected them.

Is Australia a land of forward-thinking, effort-making people who will willingly tackle any hurdle, or is it peopled by those who think mainly of their own position, and who vote themselves benefits from the efforts of others. Does our population have concerns for future generations, or is it happy to live as luxuriously as it can at the expense of those coming after them? Australia appears to now be more concerned with emotional matters such as gay marriage and climate change, two items on the daily news agenda, than with matters such as our gross debt of over $500 billion, our selling of assets to prop up our standard of living, the ridiculously unfair distribution of the Goods and Services Tax take, and the fact that Australia has lost its car manufacturing industries because our market is not big enough.

Nobody has asked why Sweden, with its population of less than 10 million with its Volvos, and the Czech Republic with its population of less than 11 million, with its Skodas, can compete on the world market, and Australia with its population of about 24 million cannot.

What is more important to the future of our country – non-heterosexuals being able to say they are married even though, until now, marriage has been the binding union of a man and a woman, or Australia being a vital manufacturing hub? We should be exploring why the established Australian car manufacturing industry could not compete on the world market, when Sweden can. Is it inefficiency, lack of technical skills, high wages, inadequate infrastructures, the higher cost of electricity and other power sources, poor management, inadequate designs, or just poor performance all round? If Australian manufacturing cannot compete, we need to know why.

If our parliaments were largely composed of those experienced in working in and managing productive businesses, as I consider it should be, such questions would, almost certainly, be asked and constructive answers arrived at. However, when parliaments are largely composed of union officials, party officers and apparatchiks of various stripes, and lawyers trained to argue a position – not people trained to solve problems – high profile sports people, entertainers, and others with recognisable public faces, and when the electorate votes for those who promise it most benefits from the taxation take, democracy is not working as it should.

Is there any chance of Australian parliaments foregoing their current wrangles to engage in thoughtful, and considered, discussion on concerns that really matter for Australia's welfare in the long term? Is it possible that they will forgo their petty one-upmanship and that the parties will only select candidates with a background of problem solving, who have intelligence and consciences, who will serve for limited periods for the overall good of Australia as a whole? I doubt it.

The productive working forces of our country need to concentrate on producing efficiently and the managers of those working forces need to lead it cost effectively. Neither group should demand rewards that are so great that our manufacturing industry is priced out of the world market. This applies especially to the rewards now expected by management. It is management who sets the demand level. The future of Australia depends on all able citizens producing more than they take.

# 17. BEING POLITICALLY CORRECT.

The days of honest discourse being stultified by the ridiculous curse of political correctness might be numbered. The election of Donald Trump to the Presidency of the US of A, despite his politically incorrect statements about large sections of the population, is one sign. The percentage of those who are tired of watching what they say, write or draw (consider Bill Leak's abysmal treatment and Israel Folau's sacking because he is a practising Christian and proud of it) because their opinion might offend some individual or group, appears to be growing.

Being honest in an opinion is not now the necessary criterion of that opinion being acceptable, as it used to be. Now we must all toe the current, politically correct line – but that, I hope, appears to be about to change.

For some time now those who feel they are entitled to act as the arbiters of what can be expressed have had the upper hand, and they will not release their grip without a fight. They have attempted to stifle free speech and doubtful humour, and have pushed through laws that give them control over a reasonably tolerant public. The righteous have imposed the belief that offense can be given. This is not so. Offense cannot be given – it must be taken.

If a fourteen year old girl called me an ape I would be flattered. I would not have a tantrum and I would not be given a high award as a footballer was. Because I am fully aware of my shortcomings, and because I do not value the opinions of many, I do not rise to the bait of intended insults. I do not take offense.

Even banter has been proscribed by the righteous. Why? What was the harm in calling a Jew a Yid, of calling an Aborigine an Abo', a German a Kraut, a Frenchman a Frog, an Italian a Ding, an English person a Pom', an American a Yank or even an Australian an Aussie dickhead? Words have no power to hurt unless those at whom they are aimed take offense. If an insult intended to wound is said, it is only successful if a wound is felt. If the recipient reacts to the insult and becomes angry or hurt, the caster of the insult has been successful.

If someone calls me an up myself shithead I smile. Their opinion is of no value to me. Why would anyone take exception to a derogatory statement that was not true or was delivered by someone whose opinion they did not respect? I repeat – it is not possible to give offense – it is only possible to take it, and taking offence should not entitle the taker to an unearned financial reward, public accolade or the satisfaction of holding up the giver of the taken offence to the cost of a legal defence or, worse still, a financial settlement to make the offense-taker go away.

Why have larrikin Australians become so precious that they are wounded by the words of others, especially the words of people they have little, if any, respect for? Why are people now so offended by what another says, especially another whose opinion on any other matter they would not give any credibility to? What has happened to *"Sticks and stones may break my bones but names will never hurt me"*? Where is the benefit to society, or even to the person who has accepted offense, in reacting to an insult? Why have people become so thin-skinned that they collapse mentally and psychologically if someone says something about them that they take exception to? Is the taking of offense the sign of a robust society, or is it a sign of a ridiculously weak society in decline?

Who benefits from the current custom of offense being taken and the offender being pursued for 'compensation' (which now really means – money)? Certainly not the accused. That person gets taken to court and, even if he or she is exonerated, their defence can be extremely costly in our expensive courts – courts that are run by lawyers for lawyers. It has puzzled me for years why lawyers are able to charge such high fees. The 'winners' are the complainant, who can walk away with money they have not earned – that they have taken from someone who has earned it – because they have taken offence and, of course, their legal advisors.

Where is the benefit to the society from these actions? Does it make us a better society for these matters to have such a high profile? Are we rewarding the right people by awarding them someone else's money because they are thin skinned?

What has happened to the Australian spirit of give and take? Where has the Aussie ability to absorb insults with a grin gone? When and why did it disappear? Is Australia a better place now that it is illegal to give offense? I, for one, do not think so. Will we get back to a more balanced approach to offense? I do not think we will as long as our political system is largely run by self-seekers, unionists and lawyers.

None of this means that I am in favour of spreading lies about others, and being able to hide behind a defence of fair comment. There is a vast difference between calling someone a Kraut or a Dago, or even an Abo, when referring to their ethnic origin, and calling them a paedophile or a rapist. And although I believe that the truth of an accusation should be a sound defence, I do not see how anyone who makes a statement that someone is a rapist or a paedophile can possibly be sure of the truth of such a claim, unless they were present when the act was carried out. So that even if it is true, it should not be said without first-hand knowledge and, if such statements are made without proof, then and only then, should it be possible to expect monetary compensation because a reputation can be destroyed by such allegations.

Statements about ethnicity, colour, stature, appearance, mental capacity, dress sense, energy levels or truthfulness might temporarily wound a sensitive ego, but they will not do any real damage, and if they are delivered by a nasty person they are best ignored. As I said previously – offense cannot be given – it can only be taken.

If we, as a society, decide that we are going to accept that offense can be given and that money is to be paid if offense is taken, it will need to be done fairly. Although I consider that calling someone a shit is a silly insult, if it is to be an offense that causes money to change hands, it is as reasonable for that 'compensation' to be paid for someone being called a white shit as it is for someone to be called a black shit.

The law must be even handed. The legal system should not produce different results because a minority has a different ethnic background, because of their culture, or because of their entrenched spiritual beliefs. The law must be framed and administered so that all Australians are treated equally. Minorities, even large minority groups who hold a voting block worth pursuing, should not be treated differently. I consider that all Australians are just that, Australians, and that no group should be treated differently because of their colour, their religious beliefs, their ethnic background or their sexual proclivities.

I look forward to a day when offense will not be taken as readily as it now is, when an offense taker will be satisfied with an apology and will not expect an expensive and high-flown court appearance, and when it will not be considered reasonable to award sums of money to a thin-skinned, offence-taker.

# 18. MONEY AND FINANCIAL REWARDS.

I am no economist, so what I am putting on paper are the views of an engineer. They are not the esoteric and brilliant views of a skilled money person.

Money was originally conceived by most societies as a means of exchange. Goods and services were exchanged for money that could then purchase goods and services. Money was the servant of productive effort. Now it has transmuted into a commodity. Money – and its handling, has become an industry – one that absorbs a good deal of the wealth created by the productive elements of society. There appear to be far more billionaires that have made their money from dealing with money, by buying and selling, than have made their wealth from activities that are productive – that actually produce wealth.

Now that money is changing from notes and coins to figures in computers, more billionaires that have contributed little to their society will appear, and will be applauded. For reasons I do not understand, society thinks highly of those who accumulate a great deal of wealth, whereas I think highly of those who have contributed as best they can to their society.

Is a society in which the manipulators of money are more highly rewarded than those who produce our wealth, a healthy society? Is it time for western, democratic societies to critically examine their financial systems and attempt to return them to a state in which they are the servants of the wealth producing parts of those societies instead of being their masters? The recent Royal Commission into Australia's banking and superannuation systems, the Hayne commission, has shown that those who operate these systems – systems that produce no wealth – take unreasonable rewards and manipulate other people's money for their own excessive gains. This is disgraceful and ridiculously unfair.

There are basic principles of economics that are understandable. If a state decides to print a great deal of money, its value decreases on the world market and inflation sets in. Examples are the southern states during the American civil war and Germany after the First World War. So decisions have to be made as to how much money is to be put into circulation by the central banks, under the guiding hand of the government.

Another tool at the disposal of governments is the official interest rate. If a society is borrowing and spending on entertainments and non-productive elements – colosseums, theatres, other non-productive edifices, high living, luxuries – and is not producing at a rate that will support that expenditure, the interest rate can be raised to stifle the expenditure. These two tools, the printing of money and the setting of the official interest rate are, I believe, known as – 'monetary policy'.

Other possible control mechanisms are the adjusting of the taxation rate, and controlling expenditure from the public purse. This is, I believe, called 'fiscal policy'. Obviously governments are reluctant to use either of the tools of fiscal policy because they are not popular with voters, unless taxation targets the rich and the large voting public is the main recipient of the expenditure from the public purse. Taxation can stifle increases in production, and gift packages from the government, given to deal with a temporary situation, can be extremely difficult to rescind.

Using these tools, governments should, theoretically, be able to control economies so that they are in balance, but there is a major hurdle they have to clear – the hurdle of what the voting public will accept. Except for the 'controlled economies', governments and their guiding, wizard economists, are not really in control. The voters are – and if the voters want the government of the day to provide them with benefits, the government will have to oblige them, or it will lose its mandate to a party that will promise access to government funds, gathered from the various taxation sources and from borrowings.

There will always be a good deal of profound discussion as to why the funds are being provided – reasons such as public works are necessary to provide jobs; the global downturn must be avoided by spending on construction; those who do not contribute to society's productive wealth have to be housed in reasonable comfort, fed properly and medicated at a reasonable level (they do vote), after all we are a rich country; public funds must be spent to save the globe from climate change that is being created by Australia's 1.3%, or thereabouts, of the global production of $CO_2$. In the end, regardless of what a government should do with its monetary and fiscal control tools, governments have to comply with the will of the electorate.

Is the science of economics sound and are its basics clear? Does it really understand how the world's economies work, and is it able to control them reasonably, or are there forces at work that cannot be controlled? Are those who are at the helms of large businesses, or major government agencies, or banks that control large sums of money, properly and reasonably rewarded, or are they overpaid? Are these controllers striving for the best long term outcomes for Australia, or are their interests primarily their shareholders' profits, and their own financial rewards, as the current banking inquiry seems to have revealed?

These are questions that need answers. If the science of economics is truly as advanced as it is supposed to be, why did it fail to predict the recent massive collapse of the housing market in the United States, why did it fail to predict the change for the better that has occurred under the regime of President Trump, and why are there such diverse opinions between the gurus who practice the dark art?

Then there is the matter of the rewards provided to the money traders, the share traders, the heads of trading conglomerates, and those who control multi-nationals that pay little tax, none of whom are actually part of those who produce wealth. Are they entitled to the astronomical rewards they gain from their involvements? Why is the head of a bank entitled to many, many times the financial reward of a dedicated school teacher or a general medical practitioner? Why is a trader of goods, shares or money entitled to many, many times the financial reward of a skillful large machine operator or a dedicated plumber? Is the present reward system balanced and reasonable?

It is my view that the reward system is not reasonably balanced and that the producers of society's wealth – the producers of our food, the manufacturers of the many things that make our lives comfortable and enjoyable, those who actually take minerals from the ground and transmute them into useful things, and the vast number of people who design, construct and operate the infrastructure that enables these primary producers to operate efficiently, together with those who dedicate themselves to educating the next generation, and those who work to keep society healthy – are more valuable than those who manipulate markets, who provide finance when it is required and who buy and sell.

This is not to denigrate the value to society of successful inventors, innovators and originators who become exceedingly wealthy, the prospectors who find valuable deposits, the developers of new medicines or more productive plants, better machines and more efficient technical approaches. With these, the financial reward can be considered a measure of their contribution. Whether these people continue to be of value to society depends on what they then do with the wealth they have accumulated. Amassing a major pile of wealth is not an action that benefits society. Using the wealth to improve society is.

Accumulating vast sums for its own sake is, in my opinion, not a worthwhile accomplishment, even though it is highly thought of by most of today's western societies. If it is the result of luck, an inspiration, popular entertainment or development of a goal, it is reasonable, but it is not reasonable if it is the product of properly doing a job, especially if it has been achieved by taking from the productive efforts of others. Once manipulators of markets were not highly regarded. Now they are given honours and access to our political leaders (sometimes for a large fee).

And the question of value arises. Is being head of a bank or an insurance group, of a major construction group, of a large legal conglomerate, of a mining company, of a trading outfit, or of a diverse multinational group, a much more difficult and demanding job than being a skilled carpenter? Are working conditions worse for these heads than for lesser workers? Do they have to expend more effort and more of themselves? If they are more used up than a normal worker then what should the reward ratio be – twice as much, ten times as much, one hundred times as much, one thousand times as much, or ten thousand times as much? On what basis should the rewards be set? Is the present system of setting them fair? Who decides on the salaries and on what basis are they decided? Do heads receiving yearly salaries and bonuses totalling many millions consider that they have really earned 200 times as much as a building labourer? Do they consider that building labourers in Australia are worth what they are receiving when they are compared to the amount such people receive in other parts of the world? Do they think, sometimes, that they are also overpaid? This whole matter of who receives what, and who deserves what, needs to be considered. It is not something that can be left to the free market when that is controlled by a limited number of self-seeking people who have their own immediate benefit as their main driving force. It appears to me that currently many in Australia are overpaid, and that those who are overpaid are not confined to union-controlled monopolies.

If governments are not really in charge and it is the demands of voters that control governments, if the primary driving force behind the behaviour of much of the Australian population appears to be to gain as much as possible from as little effort as possible, and if there are now too many making demands on the public purse, where is Australia heading and can the present course be changed?

Because such a high percentage of the population is self-centred, not society oriented, and is apparently not concerned about the longer term future, has high levels of expectation and much lower levels of performance, the government – whether it is left leaning or right leaning, liberal, conservative, green, Labor oriented or given to hunting and fishing – will continue to spend more than it receives in order to get elected. It will then announce, as it has in the past (remember Wayne Swan?), that it will balance the budget in the future as it slides further and further into debt, and the interest bill keeps increasing.

Government assets will continue to be sold until they are exhausted, or the public revolts, and those providing the loan funds will eventually decide enough is enough.

The result could be a depression that will not be able to be controlled by the government, and those currently relying on generous government handouts will find them curtailed. General standards of living, which are probably higher than we deserve, will fall, and the country will be forced to tighten its collective belts until it returns to profit. Australia has already experienced a depression and appears to be heading towards another. Is there an alternative? The answer is "yes". But it does not depend on the government. It depends on the population of our country. All Australians, especially the money manipulators, need to expect less and to produce more, until we are again producing more than we consume. Unless this happens, and on present performances it is unlikely, we will drift further into debt and a depression.

## 19. TAXATION.

Whilst realising that, as Oliver Wendell Holmes was reported to have said, taxation is the price of civilisation, and whilst agreeing with him, I do not believe our present approaches to taxation have the best possible bases. Taxation is now ridiculously complicated, time wasting and expensive to operate for both those being taxed and for those collecting the taxes.

Are there not simpler, fairer, more sensible approaches possible – approaches that are more difficult to evade for those who wish not to pay their fair share for civilisation? In the past it was possible for any wage earner or business person, in Australia, to fill out their own taxation forms. To now comply with taxation law requires accounting, legal and auditing experts, and even experts can be cowed by the complications that they face.

The complications have sired an industry of taxation advisors whose main aim is to minimise the amount of tax their clients pay. It is not an industry that I consider worthwhile, and it certainly does not add to the common good, or the common wealth, but it must be lucrative for some or it would not have so many operators and clients. Taxation advisors can be responsible for handling large sums of money, and they can be well paid for doing so, but they are not contributing to the real wealth of our society. Are taxation advisors a good thing? Is it possible to devise taxation systems that make them redundant? It is my view that better bases for taxation are possible but I obviously need help.

Not being a clever economist or taxation specialist, my views are unlikely to carry much weight, but it appears to me that there are three main streams that can be taxed – production, consumption and exploitation of naturally occurring, and non-renewable, resources – although there are other taxation sources such as company taxes, and taxing the buying and selling of businesses, that add to the matrix and the complications. I consider these should be abandoned. A great deal of the present tax take is now based on taxing production through company taxes, personal income taxes and payroll taxes. This has always appeared to me to be taxing the wrong end of the wealth chain.

Surely fairer and better taxes are those based on consumption, and on removing and selling non-renewable resources such as metals, coal, oil and gas for profit. I believe that if a select group of economists and accountants – a group whose interests were in bettering the system, not in lining their own, or their clients', pockets – could be assembled and given the task of working out better, more equitable, simpler and fairer taxation systems based on consumption and exploitation, it could be done.

But would they want to? The present, incredibly complex shambles has been created by economists, taxation lawyers and accountants, and as they are the main beneficiaries of the complex systems they have created, my suggested select group is unlikely to want to change from the present, complicated systems that keeps them employed in their lucrative, if wasteful and non-wealth creating, jobs. A simpler and fairer system might see many of them out of work and on welfare benefits. The cost of keeping taxation lawyers and accountants on welfare would need to be balanced against the cost of the intricate accounting systems now being employed and paid for. It is likely that paying welfare to those thrown out of work by a simpler system would be considerably less than the present cost of operating the complex, existing systems, which absorb the energy of many and produce nothing of value.

The Goods and Services Tax, the GST, is a consumption tax. It was politically unpopular when it was introduced. I could not understand why. The treasury needs to take money in to provide the government with funds that it can spend on things that are worthwhile, or that it considers worthwhile, and that will attract enough votes to keep it in power.

The treasury needs funds for the modern infrastructures of transport, roads, communications, power and water, for schools and universities, for hospitals, and for defence and the control of criminality, on which productive business and private users rely. The funds have to come from somewhere.

There must be a balance between collecting funds and spending or the country will accumulate debt that it cannot service, as many countries, including Australia, appear to be in the process of doing. The money for government has to have reliable sources. Taking it from consumption and exploitation appear to me to be those right sources.

However, the GST as it now operates has two basic flaws. Because it is a flat tax on all goods and services it tends to hit those in the lower economic strata harder, and it does not discriminate between the necessities of life and its luxuries.

A more equitable arrangement would have been to have goods and services broken up into bands with different GST rates applying. For the basic goods and services – basic food items, public transport, water, electrical power, the communications systems, educational items and services, health and fitness services, safety clothing, rental under $500 per week, houses less than $500,000, buildings and equipment used for manufacturing or industry, safety gear, and other necessities – the GST should be about 5%. For mid-range items – cars less than $30,000, petrol and vehicle services, tourist class air travel, fast food outlets, entertainment venues such as concert halls and theatres, temporary accommodation below, say, $200 per night, private schools, communications, building and construction services, housing between $500,000 and $1,000,000, and clothing – the GST should be about 10%. For lower level luxury items – cars between $30,000 and $100,000, rentals over $500 per week and accommodation between $200 and $1,000 per night, business class air travel, alcohol, restaurants, housing that costs between $1,000,000 and $5,000,000, pleasure craft that cost less than $100,000 – the GST should be in the range of 20%. And for super luxury items – cars over $100,000, pleasure craft over $100,000, private aeroplanes, accommodation over $1,000 per night, houses that cost over $5,000,000, and first class aircraft accommodation, for example – the GST should be about 30%.

I realise that my suggested approach has its complications, and it will not be acceptable to those who deal in luxury items and expensive houses, so it will have many wealthy critics. I also realize that there will be those who try to fiddle with the prices and classes of their goods, services and property so that they appear to be in a lower taxation area, and that some will succeed in rorting the system, but properly utilised it will do away with the time wasting complications of income tax and the iniquitous payroll tax, and add a tax burden onto those who are best able to afford it. Also it is very difficult to avoid.

The wealthy can reduce their major tax costs by travelling tourist class and staying in basic accommodation, by not purchasing luxury boats and cars, and by not building extremely expensive residences, but that would take some of the joy out of being rich, and then they would have to find something useful to do with their wealth, so the country would become more prosperous.

Matters such as how foreign workers are to be treated have to be considered. It is my understanding that many spend as little as possible and send any money they accumulate back to their home country, so the only tax for which they will be responsible is the tax on accommodation, any services they use and food. It is probable that these lowly paid people would pay little tax and this might not be a bad thing. It needs discussion.

There is also the problem of those who purchase their expensive items overseas and bring them to Australia. This would have to be dealt with by the re-introduction of unpopular import duties.

I recognise that before such a scheme can be introduced a good deal more study will have to be undertaken to arrive at a proper balance and to avoid many problems. Any new system will have to be phased in over a period (5 years?). What I suggest is a fairer, simpler system that is less open to tax dodgers and that average workers and wealth producers will be able to understand.

It is possible that there are other, superior and simpler systems for taxing consumption than those I have suggested. What I want to see is a simpler and fairer system than the present income tax system, a tax that is less subject to avoidance, and provides tax collection that is less complicated for tax payers and their tax advisors, and reduces the huge and costly taxation department of over 20,000 employees.

## 20. COMPLICATIONS AND COSTS OF THE TAXATION SYSTEM.

Is Australia's taxation system becoming too complicated in unnecessary ways, or is it just that I have trouble comprehending the complex mess? When I joined the labour force in 1953, nearly all of us filled in our own taxation forms. Now those of us with the simplest of earning capacities need advisors – tax accountants, superannuation lawyers and independent auditors.

In the taxation department there are skilled accountants and taxation lawyers writing abstruse taxation laws, updating superannuation rules and requiring independent audits, all aimed at catching those who avoid paying tax and all costing ordinary taxpayer's time and money. Although they appear to fail to catch the big avoiders they certainly make life more difficult for most of us.

These complex laws are then studied by clever accountants and lawyers outside of the department to find ways around the laws for the financial benefit of their clients and to earn their high fees. It is an expensive and time-wasting game that absorbs energy that could be put to better use. As the years go by, the taxation law book, the taxation department's Bible, gets thicker and more complex, and both sets of experts – the government's and the taxpayer's – grow in number. They get busier and busier, and the great mass of taxpayers understands less and less of the systems with which they have to comply. (And I do not think that it is only we peasants who do not understand the complications of the system – neither do many of those who operate it).

Is this sensible? Is this present method of controlling the collection of tax (and of ensuring that the working force has adequate superannuation) the best that our society can devise? Surely there are other, simpler and fairer possibilities that intelligent, unbiased accountants and lawyers can devise – lawyers and accountants not primarily interested in their own immediate rewards but in the financial health of their country.

There is also the cost of the present systems of taxing production to be considered. According to Google the Australian Taxation Office, (ATO), employed over 20,000 people in 2016. That number is unlikely to have decreased. I have no figure for the number of those outside the ATO engaged in the business of taxation, but a conservative guess would be twice that number or 40,000. This means that some 60,000 people are spending their working lives in the unproductive pursuits of either attempting to maximise the government's taxation take, or attempting to minimise their client's taxation expenditure. Neither of these activities creates wealth.

Assuming, conservatively, that the average wage of those involved is $150,000 per annum and that their overhead costs – office accommodation, secretarial services, general office equipment, computers, communication services and profits – double that figure, the total cost of running the system would be $18 billion each year, or approximately $700 for each woman, man and child in Australia. Because the figures I have used are only educated guesses they can probably be criticised, but the issue is not in quibbling about details – it is that the taxation system is very ponderous, and very expensive. Is it the best that humanity can devise?

Those of you who have read *"Taxation"* will know that I am in favour of taxing consumption, not production, and that I advocate simpler and more understandable systems of collection. However I realise that the present system is not only deeply entrenched, it is also a system that suits those who manage to avoid paying their fair share of tax and the many who are responsible for operating the system.

Many have developed methods of avoiding paying a fair share of taxation, and their advisors make a handsome living from dealing with its complications. Major companies can arrange their costs so that they make no profit in Australia, but send their profits to countries where taxation is lower. Many of the finest financial brains are engaged in minimising taxation for those who are best placed to pay taxes to meet the costs of their society, and to help support those less able or fortunate. I repeat that the large amount of brain power, and time, that goes into the complexities of taxation, produces exactly zero real wealth.

Why has the avoidance of taxation and the pursuit of the avoiders by the taxation department become such a complex and expensive game? Why do those who have been well rewarded by the society in which they live try to avoid paying into the taxation pool, and why do those who receive money from the government (I understand that over 50% of the population now receives such benefits – at 86 I am not one of them) consider it a right, not a privilege, and go out of their way to obtain as much as they can? Why are so many Australians, a society of people who once saw themselves as being proudly independent, now happy to be takers and resist being providers?

Is it because they know that upper level civil servants and the CEOs of government, and private companies, are paid so ridiculously handsomely? The past CEO of the Australian Post Office, the government's failing postal business that is, for now, propped up by a parcel business, was paid $5.6 million in 2016. Is it because upper level civil servants in positions of trust are forced into resigning because family members appear to have taken many millions from the public purse? Is it because politicians who are charged with governing are found to be corrupt and have been lining their own pockets with millions or taking ridiculously expensive helicopter flights on our taxation money? Is it because there is little trust and the Australian society has developed into a dog eat dog mentality? Will we return to being a society that respects honour and does not admire and applaud those who accumulate vast sums, even those who have accumulated these sums by doubtful activities?

As you who have read *"Taxation"* will be aware, I agree that taxation is the price of civilisation. Those who are able should be proud to help meet the costs of their society. However, for us to be able to agree with our taxes being collected and re-distributed, the system needs to have two characteristics. It must be reasonably fair and it must be understandable. In my view the present system does not have these characteristics and, also in my view, taxation should also be based on consumption, not production.

It is now past the time that taxation laws and systems should be clarified and simplified so that they are fairer, do not penalise production and encourage taxpayers to meet their share of the costs of civilisation. They should also be framed in a manner that makes it difficult to avoid paying a fair share.

## 21. POWER, WEALTH AND THE FUTURE.

Does the gaining of power and/or wealth – the controlling of the vast power of a dictator such as Hitler or Stalin, or of a great deal of money – provide a life of fulfilment? Do luxurious living conditions, having servants and sycophants, collecting precious artefacts and being treated with deference – provide satisfaction? Does the wielding of power, or the possession of great sums, give those who have them a sense of achievement or are they really only sops to meet deep seated, and not very admirable, cravings that drive some humans? Are strivings for power or wealth worthwhile pursuits, or is wealth or power necessary to prop up weak psyches? They certainly appear to be desirable given that so many intelligent people spend their lives attempting to gain power or to accumulate wealth – but are they really?

As I have reported elsewhere in these essays (See *"Striving for Wealth"*) I believe that if wealth is accumulated as a by-product of endeavours that add to humanity's welfare, that has been gained through fortunate or clever discoveries, that comes from entertainment or art that people enjoy, or that is simply a windfall, I consider that wealth to be reasonable. I do not consider wealth accumulated from manipulating markets, artificially creating monopolies, asking for extortionate rewards for providing services or necessary goods, or otherwise stealing from society – from the public that should be being served as reasonably and as economically as possible – is admirable. And I do not believe it is fulfilling for the perpetrator.

Despite the fact that I consider that taking more than is earned is not fulfilling, striving for wealth or power appears to be a motivating force for many humans. Do these motivating forces result in advantages to humanity? Do they create conditions in which society can live together peacefully? Or are they detrimental?

In the past, and even now, seekers after political power have caused, and are continuing to cause, conflicts that have resulted in the slaughter of many. Fairly recent examples are Adolph Hitler, and Joseph Stalin, both of whom used dictatorial powers to conduct pogroms and wars that resulted in the deaths of many millions. I wonder if they found the results of their leadership fulfilling. More recently the Chinese were subjected to a famine induced by Chairman Mao that killed more than 45 million between 1958 and 1962. Today both the Chinese leader for life, Xi Jinping, and the hereditary leader of North Korea, Kim Jon-un, appear to be firmly in power and not afraid of armed conflict. Where will they lead their energetic peoples? Based on how their forerunners, Hitler and Stalin, behaved they will gradually push further and harder until the world around them reacts violently.

Whether or not this results in armed conflict is unclear. Xi, especially, will realise that there will be no triumphant victors from a nuclear war, so it is likely that he will use the prodigious energies and abilities of his vast following to gradually take over the wealth producing activities of the rest of the world by buying them. This might not be a bad thing for the populations of Africa, South America and even the western nations, although it is likely that those leading the countries being financially overwhelmed by China will resist. If western countries are to retain their sovereignty they will need to compete with the energy of China and not allow their assets to be bought to sustain lifestyles that have not been earned.

What humanity needs is leaders interested in its long term welfare, and who have the foresight to provide challenges for their populations that do not lead to armed conflict. What humanity does not need are seekers after power for its own sake as leaders. Unfortunately I find it difficult to believe that balanced, knowledgeable, thoughtful and clever leaders will arise in either the less developed countries of Africa, South America or Asia or, on the present showing, in the 'advanced' western countries. As you can see I am not optimistic about the future of the world based on past history, but it is still possible that leaders will arise who are driven by an ambition for a contented, prosperous and productive future, and that they will lead the populations of our limited globe to a peaceful, balanced and fulfilling future.

Although how the world's leaders comport themselves is probably the most important issue of this time, unless leaders have followers who are prepared to behave honourably there will continue to be friction that will inevitably lead to violence. If general prosperity and compatibility are to reign as our world advances it is necessary for humanity to behave with balance and honour. This means that one of the driving forces that motivates many – greed – will need to be, at least, minimised. Humanity will need to learn that taking more than is earned cannot be tolerated if the world is to function peaceably. The urge to accumulate wealth will need to be sublimated to a positive urge to contribute to society in some way. It is quite likely that this is an impossible dream and that parts of society are so compounded that those parts will continue to take more than they earn so that friction arises.

There are those who believe that the turmoil of conflict is a driving force behind human ingenuity and that prolonged peace leads to humanity becoming stagnant and lacking the drive for inventiveness. If this is so, and humanity needs the impetus of conflict to create, then humanity, given that it now has access to the Promethean fire of nuclear fission, could well be on its way to extinguishing itself. Or perhaps humanity will relapse into a more or less moribund state as foreseen by H. G. Wells in his book *"The Time Machine"*.

Which way will we go – in the direction of education, peaceful endeavour, population control, reason, building a better world and fulfilling humanity's potential – or will base human drives of greed, avarice and disregard for others lead to destruction?

# Issues and Challenges

# SECTION 3

# SOCIAL ISSUES

There are many facets to the manner in which the society of Australia, and the societies of the world generally, conduct themselves that, in my opinion, need thought and discussion. In this section I provide what many will consider to be my idiosyncratic views of several of them, hoping that this will lead to mature consideration by superior minds. They are in the order that I thought of them. They are not generally in order of importance, but I do consider balanced education, especially of the young, by dedicated, knowledgeable, unbiased and thoughtful teachers to be of the first importance.

## 22. EDUCATION.

A vital element for a productive society, in many ways the most necessary element, is balanced, and unbiased, education. Benjamin Franklin said, *"An investment in knowledge pays the best dividends"*, and I agree. For education to be successful it requires two ingredients – students who wish to learn, and skilful and dedicated teachers with a balanced knowledge base who impart their knowledge in an impartial manner. An education system that imparts balanced knowledge to enthusiastic students not only provides the abilities that a society needs for a peaceful, united and worthwhile future, it can also lead to the young realising their duty to their society, and wanting to be part of, and building, a decent and prosperous society. Teaching ancient fables or biases is not education. Teaching the need for ethical behaviour, passing on the history of the shortcomings of humanity, giving the young the opportunity to discover the wonders of mathematics and the sciences, providing the means for clear communication, and teaching that each individual has a duty to contribute to their society as well as they are able, is what education should do.

Learning is not easy. It requires concentration and sustained effort. Just as all bodies have different natural abilities, different strengths, different reaction times, flexibilities and senses of balance that vary, so do minds vary, so that different minds need different stimuli, and are more adept in different areas. Perhaps the most important lesson that education should impart is that each individual has a duty to use the talents each possesses to the best of their abilities. They should learn morality. Students must learn to do the best they can with their natural abilities and those with superior learning abilities should be regarded highly.

In Australia we currently live in a society in which the young with latent athletic abilities are encouraged to work on and sharpen those abilities and are given opportunities to do so, but young minds are often not given the same enthusiastic encouragement. Being intelligent is often not thought of highly by contemporary society. In fact Australia appears to be, and is, heading further down the academic scale when compared with the rest of the world and the only encouraging news is that Finland, which ranks high on the world list of academic excellence, does not require students to do homework, suggesting that it might be homework that is causing our demise.

This is obviously ridiculous, in my experience. All students will improve with effort and practise, just as all athletes improve with exercise and practise, and elite intellects must be encouraged to train, just as elite athletes are encouraged to train. Both those not equipped with superior intelligence, and those without marked athletic ability will benefit and improve by training, and should be encouraged to train.

People develop at different rates, and have different skill potentials, so there is always potential for improvement. All students should be taught that they have a duty to make the most of the talents they have, and that those who meet this challenge are worthwhile citizens. Those who refine and use their talents for the betterment of society are heroines and heroes. Those who waste theirs are a drag on society.

As I have already said education must be broad and balanced if it is to be successful. Education that teaches biases – political biases, religious biases or historical biases – without providing the various possible views of any position, is not education, it is indoctrination, and will continue to lead, as it does now, and as it has in the past, to different societies and religious groups warring with each other.

I cannot put a great enough emphasis on the value to a healthy society of education – of teaching the young the basics of language and writing, the pipelines to knowledge and to other citizens; of mathematics, the measure of so many of the natural phenomena with which we live and a great brain building exercise; of history with its lessons both good and bad, on which we can build for a more stable and useful future; of religions with their varying answers to the correct operation of society, and of the relationships between the different parts of society; of physics and chemistry so that students can gain some understanding of the way the world around them functions; of botany and biology so they can gain some knowledge of where humanity fits into nature; of astronomy and the wonders of the universe; of literature so that the lessons of the past and the variations of human nature can be learnt; of art that can show some of the higher aspirations of humanity; of the wonders of medicine and healing; of humankind's many inventions; of the built world, to show what humanity is capable of; and of human relations so that we can develop systems that enable us to live together in peace and prosperity. Most importantly, we need to teach the young that for the present welfare of the world, and for the welfare of future generations, they must behave morally.

I realise that education in the wrong hands is a tool that can lead the innocent young into what I regard as evil. When I see videos of young Moslems – boys, not young men – singing about fighting the Jews and carrying out Jihad for a Moslem world caliphate ("God willing") – and swearing to be a suicide fighter for the sake of Allah, I am sickened, and realise that education of the wrong sort can lead to further problems, not to solutions.

I repeat – we need students who wish to learn, who wish to maximise their natural abilities, guided by scholars/teachers who understand their subjects, are not misguided by any religious doctrine, and are able to impart their knowledge with enthusiasm. Do we have them? If not, we must develop them.

.

## 23. THE PATH TO PROSPERITY.

If a society aims to be prosperous it must follow a path to prosperity. To follow that path requires that the preponderance of the members of the society contribute to the welfare of their society to the best of their abilities. Although it has become lost in the maelstrom of political spin doctoring, the prosperity of a society is not achieved by any particular political system or by those selected to lead – although both can have a major effect and can act as catalysts for the achieving of prosperity – it is achieved by a high percentage of the population, a percentage that is as high as possible, contributing to the output of their society and a low percentage, a percentage that is as low as possible, taking from their society while not contributing, or contributing little. Prosperity is not created by the intelligentsia or by the leaders, although both can help create the environment that will lead to prosperity; it is created by the productive masses doing their best.

Of course the innovators, the inventors, the thinkers and those who lead the way have an important role, but if the great bulk of the people are not behind them, if the population does not strive for prosperity, it will not generally occur, although isolated sections of the community might thrive.

A prosperous society is one in which the majority of the individuals that form that society are healthy, are interested in the longer term welfare of themselves, of other members of their society and of future members of that society, are reasonably fed (not overfed, being overweight can detract from performance), wish to be, and are, broadly educated, are reasonably housed in properties that they maintain, and are, above all, enthusiastic about contributing to the common good, not because they believe in charity but because they realise that only by doing their best will their society thrive.

Prosperity of a society is not gained through the activities of the rich and powerful, although many of that group believe in their own importance, it stems from the preponderance of the citizens of that society putting in more than they take out. The glories of Rome were not built by the patricians but by the workers and masons of its society. Germany's wonderful recoveries after its defeats in World Wars 1 and 2 have been due to the population falling in behind new leaders, and energetically building autobahns, machines and cities, and developing new technologies and cohesive societies. We should all learn both the positives and the negatives from these examples. A prosperous society is built from the bottom up – not from the top down – but a prosperous society is not necessarily a good and long lived society if it tries to dominate, as Hitler's Germany did in the 1930s. To build long lived prosperity requires that a society must find new challenges, it must produce more than it consumes, and it must concentrate on producing the cake of wealth – not on how that cake is divided.

My view of what constitutes a path to prosperity will be regarded as utopian nonsense by many, and many will consider it an impossibility given that individuals in our society appear to have as their first aim their own immediate welfare, but if people do become more public-spirited and choose to do their best without being demanding, they will find that they are more satisfied with themselves because they are producing, and that, as time goes by, their own circumstances are improving as standards improve.

This, I believe, is what is driving the remarkable improvements in living conditions in China. Prosperous and happy societies are built on all, or at least the vast preponderance of, their citizens pulling their weight, as best they can. They are not built on a system that is based on the satisfying of immediate and shallow demands.

Where is Australia sitting in the prosperity stakes? Is the general population pulling its weight as best it can, or does it have high expectation levels and medium to low performance levels? What needs to be done to change the citizens of Australia from a mass that is mainly striving for immediate benefits, into a group that pulls together to produce a more prosperous future for their nation? Could education change the approach of the general population, and the demands of militant union leaders, overpaid executives, poorly performing manual workers, self-important officials and those sponging on society in different ways? Would balanced education raise the endeavours of the general population so that our prosperity grows, or are we doomed to slide further down the prosperity curve? We already owe over $500 billion, or approximately $40,000 for each Australian worker.

## 24. THE CREATION OF WEALTH.

For a society to create wealth – not for sections of a society to just accumulate it, but to actually create wealth – requires that a society efficiently, effectively and economically produces one or more of the following:
- Things that grow that can be eaten, used in construction or in producing useful products;
- Minerals needed by industry, to produce usable energy, or for making things society requires;
- Manufactured goods that are competitive and in demand.

The basic creators of wealth are growing and harvesting things, digging things up and making things. (Thank you Glen).

To become wealthy, a society must first produce food in a sustainable manner, it must efficiently exploit any mineral wealth it has that is needed by the rest of the world, and it must produce ideas, affordable energy, articles, machines, equipment, efficient transport and distribution systems of different types, clothing, and communication systems that the world also needs.

To produce these economically requires that the society has and maintains infrastructures that are efficient – transport systems, power production and distribution systems, clean water storage and distribution systems, waste product handling and re-cycling systems, and communications grids, educational establishments that provide a range of courses aimed at equipping students with knowledge that will enable them to contribute and that will instil into the students their responsibilities to their society. It also requires a health system that keeps its producers of wealth able to fulfil their duties, sound, balanced, economical and fair financial systems, and an understandable, fair and affordable legal system.

Most of all, what is needed is a society that consists of people who want to produce and who willingly take on the task of producing whatever it is they are producing in competition with other societies.

For good or ill, there is now a world market, and no society can prosper in the longer term by building a tariff wall around itself and attempting to live within that wall, so we must all recognise that whatever we do is being done in a competitive, world market place. Therefore a society, or any part of a society, cannot expect to permanently achieve a higher standard of living than societies with which it trades, except by being more efficient and by putting more effort into its production of wealth producing items. What is not needed for the creation of a society's wealth are individuals or groups whose main aim is the lining of their own pockets. This means that if sections of a community, or individuals, attempt to manipulate markets by applying monopolies of any type (rare materials, food or goods, labour markets, trade restrictions), or by otherwise unfairly limiting free markets, what is being done might temporarily benefit the manipulators financially, but it will be detrimental to a society's total wealth in the longer run because it sets an example to the shallow and greedy that is opposite to the necessary ethos that is the only way in which real wealth can be achieved – by everyone producing as well as they can.

This is not to say, as many believe, that a society will suffer from a large portion of a society's wealth falling into the hands of a single entity. Whether this is detrimental or beneficial to a society depends on what the holder of the parcel of wealth does with its parcel. If the holder uses the wealth to efficiently produce food, minerals, energy or manufactured goods, society will benefit. However if the holder uses it to indulge in an expensive lifestyle, builds personal monuments and/or purchases expensive toys, especially toys created by other societies, the holder will be detracting from its society's wealth.

What those in any society, who are not part of the groups who create wealth and who act in peripheral or non-productive ways, should realise, is that the benefits they gain come from the productive efforts of others. Because of the manner in which our society is constructed, it is possible for those who are not involved in wealth production to accumulate considerable wealth. They should realise that they are not wealth producers. There are many who are extremely well rewarded financially, who gain wealth because of the systems under which our society operates, and who consider that they are entitled to their high remunerations. But it is clear to me that those who manipulate markets, those who advertise and market the goods produced by other societies, legal advisors, financial controllers and advisors, bankers, insurers, the many and varied sportspersons and entertainers, politicians of all types – all those involved in occupations not involved in food and water, mining, energy production, efficient infrastructure, or making things – are dependent on those who are involved in wealth creation, and those who provide the infrastructures, education and health controls that make the production of that wealth possible.

I am not saying that a society does not need people administrating systems, applying and administrating laws and providing entertainment, but their roles are, by their nature, dependent on the wealth producers and perhaps they should not be – as they now appear to be – the more important and better paid parts of western societies.

There are, of course, several areas of activity that are not directly involved with wealth production that are vital if a wealthy society is to be achieved. In no particular order of importance they are health management; the design, construction and management of infrastructure; balanced education; a fair political system; fair, economical and balanced legal and justice systems; and financial systems that look after what is, after all, the public's wealth and that invest it wisely, without claiming excessive rewards for doing so. The wealth producing activities and their necessary supporting activities should be carried out under thoughtful and fair rules of morality.

## 25. THE HEALTH SYSTEM.

If a society is to be productive it is necessary that as large a proportion as possible of that society is healthy, and is able to contribute to the society's production. Therefore a health system that encourages healthy lifestyles and that can tend to those damaged by accidents or other misfortunes is a vital ingredient.

However, there must be limits. A health system that encourages wanton use of its facilities, many of which are extremely expensive – that has a controlling bureaucracy that absorbs a high percentage of the total health budget, and that requires excessive amounts from the public purse to tend to those who live unhealthy lives – unfairly detracts from a society's prosperity. Drug addicts, thieves, violent criminals and those who do not wish to contribute, but expect their society to support their health must nonetheless be given the benefit of the health system while they recover, but it is unfair on the productive elements of society for these non-productive people to continue to receive medical treatment if they continue their destructive lifestyles.

I realise that curtailing treatment will be considered by many to be too harsh, but to allow those who could contribute, but will not do so because of their chosen lifestyle, is quite unfair. A stance must be taken against any of those who wish to make unfair use of society on a long term basis. How this difficult matter can be reasonably resolved needs consideration and agreement. Those who are involved in operating the complicated health system, with its overtones of what constitutes 'humanity', have a duty not to overuse the facilities provided by the system, on one hand, but to do their best to keep the ailing as healthy as possible, on the other hand. It is unlikely that there will ever be agreement as to where the balance point should be.

There is no doubt in my mind that any effort to control the health system's expenditure by some outside agency will fail. The only way for reasonable control of health's costs, that will work, is a system generated by the health cohort itself. It must act as its own auditor, and not spend either needlessly, or excessively, for doubtful benefits.

At this time in western societies there is a demand by the health system for extremely high quality accommodation for both research facilities and for patients being tended – accommodation that has high quality services and expensive and technically advanced equipment and fittings. Very large sums are being spent on pieces of equipment, displays to educate the public and buildings that are architecturally impressive, with finishes that are of extremely good quality. And the whole is controlled by a bureaucracy that, itself, has a high, ongoing cost. As any patient will know there are many forms to fill in and many signatures required. Just who these pieces of paper are designed to protect – the patient, or the health system – I do not know.

Whether some of these costs are altogether necessary for the efficient operation of the health system could, and should, be questioned by those controlling the system. Because the system is largely funded from the public purse, and because those who are ill or have an affliction expect the very best of treatment, the system should be as efficient as it can be. It should limit its expenditure to those areas that are necessary. It does not need to spend public funds on excessive public spaces, with fancy screens advertising its successes, or on architectural excesses. It should avoid spending on items, facilities or systems that are not central to its tasks of healing the ill and researching for cures. The health system does not need to advertise except by producing a healthy society.

There is no doubt that many of the health professionals and researchers are heroes and heroines of society and are to be applauded, but there is also the possibility of a self-serving bureaucracy that needs control from within. The matter of the preservation of life is a very emotional one, so I will not enter into it here except to say that if and when I reach the stage of not being able to reasonably fend for myself, I wish to die peacefully. I do not want to be kept alive and moribund at the expense of my society.

# 26. INFRASTRUCTURE AND POWER PRODUCTION.

The design, construction and operation of a complex infrastructure that supports the production of food, minerals and manufacture is vital for prosperity. Without economical production of electrical power and an efficient distribution system; clean water storage and distribution; an efficient communication system that has a wide network; an economical transportation system with its necessary railways, roads, bridges, overpasses and efficient vehicles; living and working accommodation; and handling and recycling of waste products to minimise pollution, the wealth producing sections of our society would not be able to operate properly. The designers, managers, operators and day-to-day workers of our infrastructure systems are the unsung heroines and heroes of our society.

An important element of modern society's infrastructure – perhaps the most important single element for the civilisation that has developed, for mining and for manufacturing, and one of its most controversial – is the production of electrical power. It was the harnessing and production of electrical power that enabled our world to rise to its present state of affluence and comfort, and was central to raising its standards of living.

When humanity discovered fire it became possible to make things from metals, to be kept warm and to cook food, which sterilized harmful bacteria.

Coal was found, and it was later used to create steam which powered machines, and later again it led to the production of electricity. More recently, the use of other fossil fuels, oil and gas, has been developed to meet the growing need for more and more electrical power. The appetite for more electrical power increases as the world's population increases, and as standards of living rise, but whether we humans can continue to burn ever increasing amounts of fossil fuels into the future, without affecting the earth's climate, is now open to doubt.

Whether changes in the Earth's climate, brought about by increasing $CO_2$, will be detrimental or beneficial has yet to be agreed, but the general emotional response appears to be that any change will be for the worse. One factor that will limit the continuing use of fossil fuel to produce our heat and power, even if it is found in the future that increasing $CO_2$ is not the detrimental monster it is now being made out to be by some, is that no matter how vast the store of fossil fuels is, that store is finite. It will not last forever. Another is the politically and emotionally sensitive matter that the burning of fossil fuels increases the $CO_2$ in the atmosphere, with its unknown long term effects. Will the increase of $CO_2$ make changes to the climate that are deleterious or beneficial? Certainly the climate has changed quite markedly, and quite quickly, even during recorded history.

A recorded change that has taken place – before the major burning of fossil fuels – is the Medieval Warm Period (950AD – 1250AD). It was during this period that Eric the Red found and farmed a new land that he named Greenland because it was green, and semi-tropical fruits grew in northern England. The Medieval Warm Period was followed by the Little Ice Age (1300AD -1870AD) during which the Thames froze over. There are arguments as to the causes and effects of these changes, but there is no doubt they occurred.

Were they due to changes in the inclination of the Earth's axis or its orbit around the sun? Is the main driver of climate change sun spot activity on our heat source, our sun, or is it humanity's production of $CO_2$? Is volcanic activity a major contributor? Will increased $CO_2$ cause plants to grow more luxuriantly as they absorb the $CO_2$ from the atmosphere, providing an increase in food supply and in future stores of energy? Will areas that are now deserts or are now frozen become arable and vegetation friendly as they once were? Will they then create more coal, oil and gas, as they have under the desert areas of the Middle-East in the past?

Will rising temperatures cause the oceans to rise and swamp low-lying islands? Will the coral reefs of the world expire, as considered likely by those who want to abandon the consumption of fossil fuels? Will large parts of the globe that are now inhabitable become uninhabitable or will more of the globe that is now uninhabitable become inhabitable?

There are many questions to which we do not yet have answers. Based on the history of the past a warming phase is certainly preferable to another Little Ice Age – an ice age similar to that of the 17$^{th}$ century – as predicted will occur by some scientists.

Other questions are – should Australia with its estimated, approximately 1.3% - 1.4% of global CO2 production be attempting to expensively cut its production of what might really be a useful addition to the atmosphere when its CO2 output has a negligible effect on the global total? China, India and the USA produce most of the world's CO2 and they are increasing their productions of it. Have the long term effects of increased CO2, been sufficiently studied, or has the western world been led into accepting that it is an evil by the emotional appeals of the Al Gores of this world, and their scientific backers who receive remunerations and doctorates for their investigations?

Apart from electrical power production CO2 is produced by the consumption of fossil fuels for the ever growing transport needs of our world – our road transport, our ships, our aircraft, the huge expenditure of fuel for space explorations, and our industrial and farm machinery. Then there are our forest fires, erupting volcanoes and the CO2 and other greenhouse gases produced by the breathing and belching of the historically huge human population, and the many animals we nurture for various reasons. What are their contributions? (See *"Global Warming – Climate Change"*) Why are these sources of CO2 not attracting the same concerns as the production of electricity?

Possibly it is because those that want electrical power delivered by 'renewable' energy for emotional or (curse the thought) financial reasons, do not want to be without their steaks and chops, their ocean voyages, their flights to distant places or their personal vehicles – or am I being unduly cynical?

Until we research the contributions of all sources of CO2 and compare them, until we know just what the contribution of electrical power production by burning fossil fuels is to the total production of the dreaded gas, and until the total picture can be clearly seen, raising the costs of electrical power in Australia so that we are not able to compete on a world market is a foolish gesture. It is not only foolish, it is cynical, when we continue to send fossil fuels to other countries who burn them to produce cheap electrical power.

There are other questions that bother me. There is no doubt that the world wants more electrical power, so how is it to be produced? The current, popular means of producing that power, for reasons that appear to me to be more emotional than rational, are by the so called 'sustainable' production methods – wind, solar and wave energy. They are known to be expensive, but they are highly thought of because they do not produce CO2 – or do they?

Recent analyses by the Swiss engineer Ferrucio Ferroni has found that modern coal fired power stations emit 846 grams of carbon dioxide per kilowatt hour when run on hard coal whereas solar panels that last for 25 years produce 978 grams of carbon dioxide per kilowatt hour when all aspects of fabrication, storage and disposal are taken into account. I cannot vouch for the figures but it is clear that analyses of this sort should be made, and confirmed, before we commit to using power producers that might well make the CO2 problem worse while appearing to be a saviour. We have to know how much CO2 is produced in their manufacture, maintenance and disposal. What is the energy return period for each of these electrical power producers? How efficient are they, and how long will each take to produce the energy that was put into making and maintaining them?

I have been told by an engineer involved in the building of wind towers that it takes several years for wind towers to return the energy used in making them. He had no figures for the energy needed to maintain the various 'renewable' power sources or for their removal once they wore out. Why the information on the energy return period for wind towers and PV cells is not commonly available is a mystery to me. As an engineer it would seem to me to be the first analysis that should have been made, and made public. If it takes many years to get back the energy used to make a tower, to maintain it and to dispose of it once it is no longer useful, should they be built when they have a number of environmental drawbacks?

Are there alternatives not yet being pursued by the champions of renewable energy? What about tidal energy? What about further exploiting hydro-electric energy, even if the Greens do not like the idea? Switzerland largely relies on hydro-electric power, but it still appears to be in sound and green condition. So does Norway with its 99% reliance on hydro-electric power production.

What about the batteries that are necessary for storage to make power available during the down times for the 'renewables'? What energy will these absorb during their manufacture and maintenance? Will they leave a nasty residue when they age? Are there vested interests that are profiting or gaining political kudos from this 'green' revolution, so that their motives are not as altruistic as they seem? Should we be trying to extract heat from the Earth's mantle of molten rock under the crust on which we live? These are questions that the proponents of wind, solar and wave energy are not answering.

The power of 'renewables' must be stored in batteries for a continuous supply of electricity when the sun does not shine, the wind does not blow and the seas are flat. Will the batteries in which the energy is stored last forever, or will they have to be renewed regularly? How much power will be used to produce them and what will the energy return period on them be? If they have to be replaced, will they be easy to dispose of cleanly, or will they be polluting? I have seen no discussion on the energy consumed by the manufacture of, or the disposal of, batteries by the sustainable energy champions. We need to investigate the possible downsides to our present means of storing renewable electrical energy before we commit to it too heavily.

As I have already pointed out, the main question, in fact the overriding question, and the question I have never yet seen answered satisfactorily, is – what is the return on the energy put into making and maintaining these 'clean energy' producers? How long is it before these 'renewable energy' producers produce the power that goes into making and maintaining them and their storage systems? How long will they last? Will it be long enough for them to produce enough energy to be substantially greater than the energy put into making and maintaining them? Unless it is clear that they can produce several times the energy put into their creation, maintenance, demolition and disposal of their toxic elements, when they have reached the end of their useful lives, as they inevitably will, they are not worth having because they all have impacts on their local environments. More balanced investigation and verifiable evidence is necessary before Australia commits to what does not appear to me to be a rational approach to its future, reliable and increasing, electrical energy needs.

If the emotionally popular renewable energy producers are not the way forward, what are the alternatives? Are there any reasonable alternatives? There is certainly one electrical energy producer possible that is already being used in a widespread way, but it appears to frighten people in this country. It is, of course, electrical energy produced by uranium or thorium.

According to Google, uranium based nuclear energy now produces over three quarters of France's electrical energy (France exports power to its neighbour Germany and Germany is now considering a return to nuclear power), and about 60 new reactors are under construction around the world. It is a reliable power source, it can respond quickly to changes in demand, it is now producing about 11% of the world's power, and, during its operation it produces none of that bogey (?) $CO_2$. However building the power plants, mining the uranium and thorium, and transporting them and their used residue, does produce the dreaded gas. This could change in the future as more and more of our power is produced by nuclear reactions, and electrical vehicles and electrical tools are developed further, so that manufacturing becomes $CO_2$ free.

Of course the use of nuclear power leads us to the question – is its residue so vile and poisonous that it should not be used under any circumstances, or can the residue be handled safely? These are questions that are still waiting to be answered. Uranium based nuclear fission leaves plutonium, which is the material needed for making nuclear bombs, and which is lethal to humans and animals. The residue from thorium is not lethal and has a much shorter half-life according to its proponents. Google's experts consider that thorium (named after the Norse God of thunder Thor) has not been investigated as thoroughly as it should have been, because the governments of the USA have expended a great deal more on the development of uranium to produce electrical power, than has been spent on thorium. Thorium could be the answer to reliable, safe and economic electrical power. We shall see.

Australia appears to be caught in a classic bind. On one hand it wants to reduce its production of about 1.3% of the world's $CO_2$, and on the other it is frightened of using a power source – a source for which it has the fuel – that is slowly being adopted around the world. There are those among us who consider that our wide, brown land, with its vast open, uninhabited and stable spaces, could be the ideal repository for spent uranium. There was even one multi-multi-millionaire mining magnate who was reputed to have said he would take the residue because it would be very valuable one day. We shall see if there are changes in the public sentiment.

I am unsure why it is so unpopular here. In Japan, whose relatively tiny islands experienced the horrors of Fukushima, I understand they are re-commissioning the nuclear plants that were shut down. We, in Australia, must decide what we are more afraid of – a nuclear accident on our stable and largely deserted land, or carrying the costs of power production that is much greater than power produced by uranium or thorium, and losing industries to countries that have adopted economical, nuclear power sources.

Our alternatives appear to be to continue to burn fossil fuels until they become depleted and the $CO_2$ in our atmosphere rises to higher levels with its unknown effects, to develop renewable energy sources that really produce more energy than they absorb, and that do not have unfortunate residues and unfortunate effects on the environment, to find sources of energy that are, as yet, untapped and that can be sourced reasonably readily, or to use the frightening nuclear power and to deal with the residue. Which is the most attractive?

What is certain is that as the population of the world grows so will the demand for more and more electrical power grow. As demand grows should we also be working out less energy-intensive ways of conducting our lives, such as by cutting down on our massive use of transport, by living differently, and by building for climate control?

## 27. THE PRODUCTION OF FOOD AND CLEAN WATER.

Food and clean water are absolute necessities for the survival of humanity, and there are not too many such absolute necessities, so that the section of humanity that provides these two elements is obviously a most important part of civilisation as we know it, if not the most important part.

Yet I have gained the impression from the manner in which western societies behave that we do not value the catchers and cleaners of the fish we eat, the growers of the fruit, grains and vegetables we consume, and those who husband the animals that provide us meat and milk. They quietly meet market demands and produce our food, but they are heard from very little. The public fusses are not made about the producers but about the distributors – the Coles, Woolworths, Aldis and IGA's of society – who not only claim the limelight but also take a large slice of the profit pie. The world's population is growing by about 80 million each year, and although there are pockets of starvation in Africa brought about by excessive numbers of children and wars between religious factions, most of the world remains well fed. In fact in several of the world's western democracies many people are not eating to sustenance levels, they are eating to obesity levels.

It is my view that we should all be grateful to the scientists who have improved the qualities and production rates of our foods, those who catch, grow, reap, husband and treat our food sources so that they are hygienically edible, and last and least, those who distribute our foods for profit.

The accolades I consider due to the producers of our foods I consider also due to those who quietly and efficiently control and distribute our clean water and then dispose of the waste products humanity produces once it has used that invaluable resource. Without a clean and uncontaminated water supply civilisation could not exist as it does.

I am intrigued by the Financial Review's recent list of 21 people who are changing Australia. The list contains entrepreneurs, directors, a scientist, a TV personality, charity organisers, financiers, an economist, an art dealer, a computer technologist or two, a drone controller, the chief of a motoring organisation, a teacher, a female football club president and a militant female defender of Aboriginal rights. Not one of these is involved in the precious and necessary production of our food and clean water, and none would be able to operate if it was not for those producers. Are we, as a society, losing our sense of balance – our sense of what is important and what is not?

# 28. THE LEGAL SYSTEM.

For any society to function reasonably, especially for the complex and crowded societies that are now normal on our limited globe, an equitable legal system is a necessity. It should be such that it does not unduly trouble those who follow society's rules and contribute to it. Its aim should be to prevent, or at least dissuade, those who would take more than their legal due from their society, and to temporarily remove from society those who behave dishonestly, violently or destructively, for rehabilitation.

It should not limit the activities of those who have unusual views, unless those views are destructive, and it must be very careful about limiting freedom of speech or opinion unless either are damaging to the overall good of society.

Freedom of opinion, and publicly making opinions known, should not be limited by law if the limitation is only to prevent an opinion giving offense. Whether a statement is offensive is a subjective matter – it depends on whether or not someone finds it offensive – and laws should not be in place to decide subjective issues. Insults can be ignored, they do not have to be accepted. There must be limitations placed on damaging untruths however, and if statements are found to be untrue, there probably should be punishment. This area of law needs to be carefully considered. There is a good deal of difference between calling a person a dirty dog or a black (or white) bastard, inane statements that have doubtful factual bases, and accusing someone of being a paedophile, which might, or might not, be true.

A reasonable justice system must also be wary about relieving individuals of personal responsibility. In Australia the law appears to be moving towards finding reasons why miscreants, those who cause accidents, and law breakers, act as they do because of some outside influence – society and/or life has treated them badly, they were mistreated or bullied as a child, their forebears were treated badly, the road needed repair, they were distracted by a sign, their experiences have unsettled them – so that personal responsibility is being, unfortunately in my opinion, eroded.

This has the twofold effect of making the state responsible for many mishaps, resulting in a blow-out of cost to the public purse and, more importantly, of reducing the self-reliance of the citizens of Australia. If the road is rough or dangerous, drive more cautiously. The law should not reduce the autonomy and responsibility of the citizens, because it will reduce their much desired independence, and will lead to a soft, nanny state. A healthy state is one in which the people are proud to take personal responsibility and do so willingly.

The legal systems – the laws of Australia, the policing organisations, the legal practitioners and the incarceration edifices – are now extremely complex and expensive. They produce very little of value but they absorb a good deal of society's wealth and intelligence. Is it in Australia's interests to have so much of Australia's intelligence, especially the high intelligence required by the complexities of the law, and its high day-to-day running costs, tied up in what is an unproductive pursuit? Is our adversarial legal system the best possible system for deciding where responsibilities lie, or are alternatives that are fair, just and more equitable and economical possible? The system has now reached a point at which the cost of the legal actions in many cases can be more than the remedy. Is this sensible?

I have no solutions to these questions, but I consider they have to be asked and debated until a less wasteful system is arrived at. Under the present system there is no imperative, no driving force, for legal matters to be settled quickly. The longer a matter takes to settle, the more the legal practitioners involved are paid. This is not to imply that lawyers, and their technical advisors, deliberately spin out their cases, the good ones are always too busy to do so, but when there is no advantage in ending a disagreement in a short time and the longer a settlement takes the more those involved are paid, answers will not be arrived at quickly.

For cases of right or wrong – guilty or not guilty – perhaps the system of adversarial lawyers battling out cases before a judge, with or without a jury, should be retained, but for complex medical or technical matters, especially those that involve more than one possible offender, and in which experts are involved, perhaps the cases for the parties could be put before a disinterested expert panel, not a legal practitioner, who would then make its finding on the basis of what is practical and reasonable, not necessarily what is in accordance with statutes and the requirement for incontrovertible evidence. An expert panel would be in a much better position to understand the complexities of technical evidence than someone trained in the complexities of the law. There have been attempts to set up systems that avoid the complexities of the law – arbitration, mediation and alternative dispute resolution – but these have become overtaken by the legal system with all its complexities.

I am not advocating wholesale or immediate changes to the systems now in place. What I am advocating is that alternatives that are not adversarial and that are less complex and expensive are looked at and, if found effective, gradually developed and adopted.

## 29. MONEY.

For a civilised, functioning society to operate, it has been necessary for over 2000 years to have a value exchange system that has enabled governments to collect taxes and that has facilitated trading. Until recently that system has been money – originally coins and, more recently notes and cheques– objects with a physical presence. In the past, each country has had its own currency, and the exchange rate between currencies has been set by the world market's assessment as to how a country was performing in its production of wealth-creating elements.

If a country performed poorly, the world market degraded the value of its currency so that its citizens could not afford artefacts that other societies could. Countries with a de-valued currency became cheap to visit, so the wealthier nations took advantage of the low cost and holidayed in them. A country with a currency of low value could either accept its position in the scheme of things, or it could meet the challenge by improving its wealth-creating performance. There were forces balancing the wealth of a country against its performance.

Now there are disparate countries using the same currency so that the natural balance that could be achieved by changing the value of a country's money is no longer possible. And now there are ways of doing away with physical money, and of exchanging value electronically, with those organising the exchanges charging for their service. How this will all play out I have no idea, but I am concerned that the complexities of systems that are now in play will become avenues for the greedy to take unearned wealth from those who have earned it.

From its fairly simple beginning of facilitating the exchange of goods and labour for the money of the time, the monies of the world have become ridiculously complex. I do not pretend to understand how the world's economies now work or what will happen in the future. What I do know is that, given that a section of humanity is greedy for wealth, whatever means of exchange comes up in the future, the producers of real wealth will be exploited by money grubbers. What I also know is that there is no agreement between the money experts – the economists – so there is little chance that we will be informed of any crash before it happens.

International currencies that are not based on paper, gold or another metal are now being developed. How this will all work out I do not know. I am sure that there will be those who attempt to steal from these new currencies or profit from them. To me the Bit Coin boom smacks of Holland's black tulip boom in the $17^{th}$ century.

What the cleverest economists should be doing is working out the fairest and safest systems of value exchanging that can be readily understood, and that is difficult, if not impossible, to exploit. I do not know why a section of the population considers that taking as much as they can, and contributing as little as they can, is their best approach. If the entire population behaved in that fashion, the economies of the world would be in tatters. Economies only thrive when the bulk of the working population gives more than it takes.

# 30. PERSONAL RESPONSIBILITY.

Where has personal responsibility gone? Throughout history it has been necessary for people to attend to their own physical well-being, to rely on their own judgements in financial matters, and to make their own decisions on matters of potential hazard. People have had to decide how they travelled and how fast, whether or not they climbed trees and mountains, whether they went into battle or conscientiously objected and how they comported themselves once committed, whether they ate and drank reasonably or gluttonously, and whether they obeyed the laws of their particular God, and man, or defied them. Having made their decisions they then wore the consequences. This exercising of personal decision making and the responsibilities it brings with it is now being whittled away. Why? Is the loss a good thing?

People in western societies are now expecting to be protected from themselves. Not only do they expect to be protected, they expect that should they become damaged due to their own lack of judgement they will be provided with care and money. They will be 'compensated'. If a person is gaoled for a crime and dies in gaol due to an illness they brought with them, that person's family has been known to sue for compensation – for money – from their society. Is this even vaguely reasonable? Is it reasonable that society is made financially responsible for a death, and is it reasonable that a family benefits financially from the death of a relative? Are families really this greedy for money, or are they being encouraged by those who will fight the legal issues for them and will profit handsomely should they receive a financial settlement?

And if, in western societies, a person commits a crime that warrants punishment, they find themselves in quite comfortable surroundings; in a home from home. They are not badly housed and fed, or sent to out of the way settlements where life is hard, as they once were. They are not denied the opportunity to play various games or sports, although cross-country running is limited, and their health and well-being is attended to at the expense of their society. Their personal responsibility for the crime they have committed results only in a limitation of freedom to wander as they will for a period.

There is a growing culture in Australia of making claims for damages – for 'compensation'. It is a culture fuelled by some of the burgeoning groups of legal advisors who offer free advice for those damaged, often in the knowledge that the cost of defending a weak claim is going to be greater than a payment that can be made to settle the matter, so a money settlement is arrived at. This is, in my view, an unhealthy culture, and it is leading to false claims being made. I am not suggesting that those who have been damaged, for whatever reason, should not receive financial benefits from the public purse. They should. But they should also realise that the benefits they receive are a privilege, not a right. It is my belief that the decision as to the right and reasonable amount to be paid from the public purse to the damaged party should not be decided by the expensive, and complex, adversarial legal system but by a Board of persons with varying and long term work, and financial experiences. The present system is so expensive that it swallows a large percentage of whatever payment is decided on. This matter, the matter of the charges made by the legal profession for its involvement, is rarely reported on or discussed openly, as I consider it should be.

Getting back to the matter of taking personal responsibility. A part of our society appears to have been taking, and is continuing to take, much time and effort to find excuses for those who have caused damage to society or to themselves, that remove their personal responsibility. Why is this so, and is it a good thing? Should we be training vandals and criminals to believe they are the victims of their circumstances, or should we be making it clear that how one behaves, how one comports oneself in society, is a personal matter; a personal responsibility?

Someone vandalises property – they have been poorly parented. Someone steals from another – they have been under-privileged. Someone gets high on drugs, hurts others and destroys property – they had an unhappy childhood. Someone runs riot and kills others – they have been the victim of religious propaganda. Someone sells destructive drugs – they were poor and needed to make money. Should society accept these excuses or should it make it clear that how an individual behaves is that individual's own responsibility?

I once asked a very prominent Australian army man why soldiers, who are trained for warfare and aggression, so often turn out to be model citizens. His reply was, *"In the army we learn to obey orders and we learn discipline"*. I think that the whole of our society needs to learn both these things. We each need to learn that society does not owe something to each individual – each individual has a duty, a responsibility, to contribute to society as best they can, and each needs to learn discipline. Discipline, the training of people to comply with a code of behaviour, is now in short supply. Today the emphasis is on individuality, with all being praised for any minor accomplishment. None must be made to feel inadequate in any way. All must be special. That is, of course, not really possible.

And where do the miscreants, those who attack society, find themselves if they are unlucky enough to be apprehended? As I reported earlier in this, they go to prisons where they are often more comfortable, better fed and better looked after than they were outside prison. Prison is no longer a nasty place to be and now comes complete with games, comforts, reasonable food, single rooms, occupational therapy, health checks, camaraderie and even, in some cases, smuggled in delights. I have no wish to go to prison to exist in these conditions, because I do not want my freedom to be limited (the downside of prison), but I have certainly spent considerable periods of time in much less comfortable surroundings.

I believe that we should be telling future generations that they have a duty to perform as well as they can for their society, that they must be disciplined in their behaviour, and that they are obliged to take personal responsibility for their actions. Currently we are encouraging our young citizens to believe they are unique and important, that they are entitled to a share of whatever is available without contributing, especially if they belong to a minority group with a political voice, and that their responsibility is to themselves, not to the wider community. These beliefs, of self-importance, of being unique and of being entitled to a share of society's wealth are not beliefs that lead to a productive and healthy society.

# 31. CHARITY.

Charity – the giving of goods, clothing, food, shelter and money to those who have insufficient of one or more of these – is almost universally regarded as a good thing, and when a person or family that has accumulated wealth from their society donates a large sum to charity or to a hospital facility named after the donor they are publically applauded and awarded.

However, the major providers of charity are not rich citizens who receive acknowledgement for their donations, they are the taxpayers and ratepayers who support the several layers of government that exist in Australia, and that distribute government funds to the indigent. There are also the good Samaritans who donate anonymously out of sense of duty. The first group, the layers of government, hand out benefits from the public purse in order for their political masters to curry favour with the voting public in the hope that the grateful recipients will vote for the party that has been most generous with the taxpayer's money. The second group, those who donate out of a sense of duty and expect no immediate reward, are deserving of respect. But are their donations spent on what they want them spent on, or are large percentages of the take spent on the structure that collects them, on an international lifestyle for those in control of the structure, and on alcohol and other damaging substances by those who receive the hand-outs?

It is generally agreed that charity is a good thing, but is it an unalloyed blessing? The great Benjamin Franklin had this to say. *"I observed in different countries, that the more public provisions were made for the poor, the less they provided for themselves, and of course became poorer. And, on the contrary, the less that was done for them the more they did for themselves, and became richer"*. I think there are examples of the truth of this in Australia. Franklin also said, *"It is the working man who is the happy man. It is the idle man who is the miserable man"*. Not only are the idle miserable, those who are idle are also the source of many of the ills of society. Even though they are accepting hand-outs, the idle are impecunious, dissatisfied and envious of those who are prosperous, so it is they who steal, deal with corrupting substances, and disrupt the orderly working of their society. They can, and do, blame others for their poor position in their society, but they probably realise that their circumstances are the result of their own shortcomings, so they are deeply unhappy. Their unhappiness causes them to strike out at the society that provides them with charity, or to sink into a torpor.

Unhappiness with your own performance cannot be alleviated by charity. For those who depend on charity and are dissatisfied and want to gain some self-respect, there are only two courses open. The first is to complain that what they are being provided is less than they deserve, and the second is to change to a productive life-style and to put some value back into their society. The first might receive some temporary relief from an increased hand-out, but it is not a permanent solution, and many are unwilling to take the challenge of the second.

So is charity, as it is now practised, unilaterally good, or is it a mixed blessing, and who are the main beneficiaries? If Benjamin Franklin is correct it is not necessarily those who receive charity, who are the receivers of benefits, because it can lower their self-worth. In Franklin's view people are better off when fending for themselves, and charity reduces the necessity to do that. This is not an easy lesson to absorb, because there is now widespread belief throughout the western world that getting something for nothing is a gift worth having, and that being given something is superior to earning that something. Are the real beneficiaries of charity not the receivers, but the donors who can bask in the glow of well-earned righteousness?

I am not suggesting that charity should be abandoned, but it should be distributed in a manner that does not take away the incentive for people to better themselves, and to contribute to their society. It should not be used in an attempt to buy votes.

## 32. THE POPULATION FLOOD.

A topic that is discussed very little, if at all, by the political class is – is our planet capable of sustaining its growing population of humans and, if it is, is there a limit to that population's size, and what is that limit? These questions are not discussed by the politicians of the western world, almost certainly because the political class and the media that reports on that class's activities have no idea of the answers, and no way of arriving at sensible solutions if they find there are problems. So they hide from such major issues and, instead, concentrate on gay rights, the sins of those bedding others out of wedlock, the special treatment that should be given to minority groups and females (even though all should be treated the same), and how they can best expend the funds provided by taxpayers in order to gain votes, and favourable newspaper headlines. The question of population growth and its corollary questions are of vital interest to future generations. They are possibly matters of life or death for humanity.

According to Google, the human population of the world in the year 1900 was 1.6 billion. Today it is over 7.5 billion and it is growing by approximately 80 million each year, which could mean it is approaching plague proportions. This important matter needs serious research and serious discussion, yet it is being pushed to one side by irrelevancies.

The basic questions that need answering are – is the human population reaching a plague proportion similar to a locust plague, so that humanity will drink and eat itself into dying of thirst or starvation as locust plagues do – as considered by Paul Erlich in his book *"The Population Bomb"* (1968) – and if it has not already reached that level, when is it likely to happen? Or will the growing population reach a level at which it will start to destroy itself as the rat and mice colonies have in the experiments of John B. Calhoun as reported in his paper of 1962 entitled *"Population Density and Social Pathology"*. What is a sustainable population level? What has to be done to avoid the human plague breaching that sustainable level? Humanity must now find answers to these questions or future generations could find themselves in situations of destructive disorder.

The questions are not new. At the end of the 18th century Thomas Malthus wrote his *"Essay on the Principle of Population"* in which he theorised that the population of the world had the potential to increase to 256 billion in 200 years – that is by now. He had his critics. Then, in 1948, William Vogt produced *"Road to Survival"* in which he concluded that the human race was exceeding the planet's "carrying capacity" and that it was on a "march to destruction" in which "three quarters of the human race will be wiped out". His contemporary, the plant specialist Norman Borlaug, was then working on what became known as the *"Green Revolution"* that has fed a world population that has doubled. He was awarded a Nobel Prize.

The population problems have yet to be considered in depth. They certainly have not been solved.

Whether we like it or not, there appears to be a looming problem of too many people for the productive capacity of the planet and/or for the social amenity of the human race. If this is so there appear to be only two alternatives for humanity to avoid the number of people becoming so great that they overwhelm the productive space and amenity capacities of the globe. Humanity must increase the Earth's production of both food and clean water, or it must keep the number of people down to a figure that is sustainable, and that does not create destructive social behaviour.

The food and water problem has been dealt with successfully so far.

Thanks to Borlaug, and others, and to rising levels of $CO_2$, crop yields are better than ever, but there is, almost certainly, a limit to crop improvement, and of arable land on which to grow food crops. There appear to be sections of the food chain that are beginning to fail already, and there are pockets of populations that are lacking clean water and adequate food. How long can we go on fishing at the present rate, let alone at an increased rate? As an example the Dogger Bank in the North Sea has been overfished by the countries bordering it for many years, so its present yields are a fraction of what they have been in the past.

Does the rest of the world have obligations to the groups of those suffering from inadequate water and food when these inadequacies are due to those groups rapidly increasing their populations or indulging in warfare? This needs consideration and agreement. It is my view that poor societies have a duty to live within their own productive capacities and to limit their populations to those capacities.

There are, of course, good humanitarian reasons for the wealthy and well fed societies to help groups of the human race who are suffering adverse conditions due to nature misbehaving. Nature can cause volcanoes to erupt, earthquakes to occur, droughts to cause crop failures, insect plagues to ruin food production, and diseases to attack animals or crops on which a group is relying.

Once it is established that aid should be given the manner in which it is to be given must be decided. The alternatives are to send aid to those areas that are suffering or to move people to more stable and prosperous areas. At this time that usually means to areas of western democracy. It is my view, formed after there have been trials of both, that the first option – taking aid to stricken areas – is to be preferred. Moving disparate peoples en masse into societies that are unfamiliar to them, and that have quite different laws, customs, moralities and religions does not appear to have been successful. There are many examples of Diasporas forming in societies that have taken immigrants in, with the best of intentions, and of immigrants not being prepared to follow the laws or the morals and mores of the host society. They, instead, demand that their own laws and religions apply.

Even if we can continue to increase the Earth's productivity we will reach a limit, and even if we manage to raise production of food and clean water, overcrowding is likely to produce social problems, so we must look at the alternative of controlling numbers of people on our limited globe, or we must find other habitable planets.

Even if humanity can develop the will to control, and the means of controlling, population growth now, there are still problems. All societies consist of three layers – the young, who are dependent, the mature cohort, who are productive, and the aged, who are also dependent. The productive cohort must be numerous enough and productive enough to feed and look after the young, and the aged. In the event that there is a sudden reduction in the birth rate, which is necessary if numbers are to be controlled, there will come a period when the reduced number of the young mature, and that reduced productive group will be providing for a reduced cohort of the young but a much larger group of the aged. This is a problem that is particularly important in many of the African countries.

Because humanity is now capable of producing intelligent robots and more efficient machines, and as these robots and machines become better and better, production of food and provision of health care are likely to require less human input than they now do, but the demands on the reduced productive middle layer are likely to remain a major factor.

Then there is the problem of persuading the groups who traditionally have large families to fall into line with a reduced birth rate. There is a good deal of evidence that with prosperity and education, birth rates fall. There is also evidence that the populations of Europe and Northern America are all but stable, even with immigration. The big population growth areas are Africa, with an annual increase of some 30 million on a population base of 1.2 billion, and Asia, with an annual increase of 40 million on a population base of approximately 4.5 billion. It appears that it is the less developed, less educated and less prosperous peoples who have the largest families. There is also evidence that some religions encourage large families to expand their religion's numbers. Another issue is that several western democracies consider it a duty of their governments to help financially support families and children. This can encourage immigrants, and the less responsible, or those with a religion that encourages large families, to have several children, and it attracts the poor and poorly educated to those countries where they receive financial support, thus increasing the birth rate in a country that has a stable indigenous population. The long term effect of this could prove to be a disaster for democratic western countries as they grow larger contingents of the indigent, and of Moslems who do not want to assimilate, who want to change the basis of western law, who want to freely practice their religion with its call to kill infidels, and who continue to be a financial drain on the society they have joined. Of course, not many Moslems are radically murderous, but the acts of violence the few radicals can commit are a major concern to peaceful societies.

It is past time that humanity faced the problem of its burgeoning growth, and found solutions as to how to control the growth rate. The Swedish Professor, Hans Rosling, has shown that even if the birth rate now diminished to the replacement rate of only two children per couple, and he believes that is happening, the world population will still grow to at least 10 billion. The question is – is such a population sustainable? Will our Earth be able to provide the necessary clean and fresh water (already Mexico City and parts of Africa are not able to meet water demands), sufficient food, and reasonable social amenity for a population of that size? These old questions that Thomas Malthus first asked long ago, have not yet been answered. They have been ignored as humanity has been able to increase the production of food, but a limit will be reached. It is my belief that whether the peoples of our planet like it or not, we now have to trim population growth. The question is how? If we fail in controlling the growth, if we leave the solution in the hands of one of the Gods that give comfort to so many, as we now appear to be doing, the solution will be war and killing over the diminishing food and water supplies and starvation of the weak. God allowed the dinosaurs to be wiped out. I doubt that He or She or It would concern Itself, Herself or Himself more over the naked ape than the mighty dinosaurs. The problem of overpopulation and how it can be dealt with is not God's to solve. It is ours. We should now arrive at answers to the Earth's capacity to support burgeoning humanity or future generations could suffer serious consequences.

## 33. STRIVING FOR WEALTH.

One of the driving forces of many of the human race, that I have difficulty in understanding, is the need to accumulate as much wealth as possible. After all, any person's real needs are limited, so why do some have the urge to get a great deal more than is necessary to satisfy those needs? Is the gathering of wealth a game they feel they must win, is it to counter some shortcoming they have identified in themselves, or is it that some are born greedy and manipulative? There appear to be only five means of accumulating vast wealth – to have appearance and talent that others will pay to experience, a lucky discovery or huge lottery win, by inventing a solution to a problem that is saleable and that no-one has previously found and having the ability to commercialise it, by building a successful business, or by manipulating some market for personal, financial gain.

There are those who accumulate wealth as entertainers, others because they find a deposit of a natural resource or win a lottery, there are those who invent or produce something the world needs (or wants), and there are those who build businesses that contribute to the efficient functioning of their society. We can only cheer the lucky ones, and the talented ones who invent or produce useful things or develop businesses that help their society. They are to be applauded. What these contributing individuals or groups do with their wealth is important. If they continue to contribute to their society they will continue to be of value but if they use their wealth for ostentation and excessive luxury they are of little value, to that society. I do not understand why some regard sitting on the deck of a ridiculously expensive launch in Monaco's harbour sipping French champagne is a preferred way of filling in a life span that is really short. Surely creating things of value, or attempting to improve your society, in what is a limited life time frame, is more fulfilling.

There are those who accumulate wealth by taking rewards that are out of proportion to their input, taking unconscionable margins on what they are marketing, finding flaws in the governing rules and exploiting them, making false claims about financial and other products, dealing corruptly or stealing outright, marketing destructive materials such as killing weapons or drugs, charging exorbitant fees for their services, and generally behaving greedily with the sole aim of accumulating wealth. These people are not assets to society in my opinion, but they often receive public accolades and can be highly regarded.

My question is why? Why do intelligent people spend their lives accumulating money in doubtful ways? What is the magic in accumulating sums dishonourably? The only conclusion I have been able to reach is that such people do what they do to satisfy their greed for one of two reasons. The first is that besting their fellows gives them a feeling of superiority, and the second is that they measure their self-importance by the size of the pile they accumulate. Maybe I am being too harsh. Perhaps some see accumulation of wealth as a real life game of Monopoly and play it against the world. I would understand playing such a game, but I do not regard it as admirable.

Real wealth is not achieved by accumulating money and goods or in striving for public accolade, but in using the talents you possess for the benefit of the society in which you live. Oligarchs and billionaires are not necessarily admirable in my opinion.

## 34. INHERITANCE.

I now venture into the complicated, vexed and emotionally clouded matter of inheritance, with trepidation. I have many questions but few answers. Any answers should be the result of unemotional and balanced consideration, and need discussion and thought.

Inheritances can come in many forms – negotiable wealth in many guises, property of various types, functioning businesses, commercial undertakings, religions, educational approaches, and customs and conventions. An inheritance is a mixture of worldly goods and cultural leanings left to others by a person who has died. The questions that need to be answered are – who is entitled to receive the benefit of one or more of these valuable and cultural commodities, and why do they have the right to that entitlement? Should the society that made the accumulation of the inheritance possible be entitled to share in it, or is it reasonable that only inheritors selected by the deceased owner benefit?

Western society appears to generally agree that the decision as to who receives the benefits belongs to the owner of the legacy, and that the decisions as to where it is to go are to be made some time before death. It is also generally agreed that close relatives, normally offspring and/or partners, are entitled to be the main recipients of an inheritance, and that it is reasonable that parents and partners pass things of value onto their heirs.

This is understandable and even admirable in many ways – but is it fair? Is it reasonable that, in the lottery of life, anyone should receive as a gift a life of idle luxury as a birthright? I am torn between considering that all citizens should start from as even a base as possible, so that I am, on one hand, against an individual receiving inherited wealth or a profitable farm or business, to admiring, on the other hand, what family dynasties have been able to achieve for both themselves and their societies. There are many examples of individuals who have laid the foundations of businesses or developments on which their following generations have built greater and more successful edifices. A few disparate examples are Mark Kingdom Brunel, Henry Ford, the Murdochs and the Packers (although I have reservations about gambling being of benefit to society).

The basic unfairness of some privileged people being granted a life of idle luxury by an accident of birth is probably balanced by energetic and talented families following on from solid starts to create businesses that benefit society.

Although I am not absolutely certain, I think I believe that all citizens of a reasonable society should contribute as well as they are able. They should not be able to sponge on the efforts, or good fortune, of a relative, or on their society. They should not be able to spend their lives idly consuming, nor should they want to. Maybe western society has brought the problems of idlers and spongers on itself by showing through its entertainment outlets that a sybaritic lifestyle is one that is to be aspired to. Audiences can gain the impression that if Michael Douglas can become a multi-millionaire in 90 minutes on the silver screen, they should be able to achieve that status in no longer than a year. Are we in western societies being brain-washed into believing that true happiness is achieved by sitting in the sun on the afterdeck of a fabulously expensive yacht whilst sipping Dom Perignon? It is not. Despite the brain-washing, many still believe that true happiness comes with the satisfactions of a task well done, whether it is growing something, designing and/or making something, contributing to society by tending the ill, teaching the young, providing a public service or, very importantly, by raising a well-balanced family.

If getting something without earning it is not a path to fulfilment, is inheriting a fortune, and living on it, a worthwhile way of filling in a short life?

There is another side to inheritance that needs unemotional and balanced discussion. It is whether having forebears who were mistreated in the distant pass entitles someone to benefits provided by today's society. Can a lack of fairness to generations past be redressed by handing out funds from the public purse to today's descendants? For instance are the descendants of the Saxon nobles of England, who were displaced by William the Conqueror, entitled to special treatment? They certainly do not get it. In a fair society should descendants of a group who were conquered hundreds of years ago have as a birthright the opportunity to live off the efforts of the current society, or should the descendants of both the indigenous and the invaders all have a responsibility to contribute to their mixed society as best they can?

If there are imbalances in society, is giving money to the disadvantaged the best method of balancing the unfairness? Would a better answer be that society provides opportunities and encouragement to enhance the abilities of those who see themselves as having been mistreated, because their forebears were overrun, so they can contribute? What can be done if those complaining of a lack of fairness decide not to take the opportunities offered to become equipped with skills that would enable them to contribute to their society, and continue to complain and demand?

Then there is the matter of the inheritance of religious beliefs. On the evidence available there is little doubt that the differences in religious beliefs have been at the root of much of the devastation and killings in the past two thousand years, and they have been a major cause of much of today's worst behaviour. Israel is bombed and threatened and protects itself by killing its enemies and erecting walls, the Sunnis and the Shiites kill each other and devastate each other's settlements, Christians and Moslems battle in several African countries, Moslems are forced out of Myanmar by Buddhists, the Christians of the Philippines fight with a militant Moslem minority, and Christians line up behind a militant president in that bastion of freedom – the

U. S of A – and flourish their weapons. Why have the main religions become the sources of so much conflict? Is it because they have militantly nasty beliefs or is it just that their animosities are off-shoots of ancient tribal and racial hatreds clothed in religion? The evidence points to the fact that inheriting religious beliefs and acting on those beliefs is one of the major causes, if not the major cause, of wars on our troubled globe. It is time humanity shed these conflicting beliefs and learned to live together in helpful harmony, a harmony in which we tackle the huge problems that face us on our over-populated globe. Will we? I doubt it.

It is also time that we reached agreements as to how the financial spoils of an energetic, or lucky, life should be spread and who should receive the benefits. Should it be only the family members or should society share?

## 35. ENTERTAINMENT.

I cannot fathom why others, and I, find entertainment in many of the things we find entertaining. What enthrals us about an orchestra playing Mozart, a group of very large people throwing a sphere through a hooped net, cyclists battling fatigue crossing mountain passes, having accidents and vying with each other for days, hugely expensive cars tearing around enclosed circuits or bouncing over rough tracks, muscular young men tossing slender and agile women around in theatres (ballet) and in large tents (*Circ du Soleil*) and, especially, what keeps us glued to television screens or sitting silently in picture theatres?

Why do TV shows of cooks and their concoctions in various parts of the world attract large audiences? Why do we pack into uncomfortable grandstands to watch young men and women attempt to get an oval ball between tall poles? What is the attraction of watching people pummel and wrestle each other? Why do we attend controlled displays of explosions on Australia Day en masse? And why have we become addicted to television?

I more or less understand why we watch intelligent humans present information about parts of the world with which we are not familiar (who can resist David Attenborough's charms?) and why we watch the news (to stay up to date with the troubles of our globe). I even understand why we watch quiz and game shows (perhaps we will learn something).

What I do not understand at all is why we are so attracted to murders and violence and find satisfaction in watching detectives catch criminals. Why do we find crime so involving? Perhaps our interest in crime tells us something about ourselves – but what?

Tastes change. Who would sit through *"Have Gun Will Travel"* or be enthralled by *"Top Team"* on black and white TV these days? It is likely that many, if not most, of today's popular TV shows will also be consigned to the bin of history when three-dimensional television becomes the norm. Maybe we humans will stop finding most comedians funny. I know I have, and I cannot fathom why Abbott and Costello once caused me to laugh.

There are many different forms of entertainment of course, and different appreciations of those forms by different people. Ballet, which was once an entertainment that was widely popular, is now an entertainment for the dinner suit and long dress set. So, to a large extent is opera, except in Italy, where it still attracts large crowds of ordinary people. Jazz, once considered the inferior music of an inferior people, has been lifted into the upper echelons of good taste. These days the tuneless gabble of hip hop is the voice of many of the young, while leaving me extremely unimpressed. I doubt that it will ever be lifted into the lexicon of high taste as swing and jazz have been.

The point I hope I am making is that humanity, at different times and under different circumstances, find different things entertaining, and tastes change. I do not understand what leads to these changes. I would like to know what makes things entertaining. I was once enchanted by technicolour films, by Nelson Eddy and Jeanette McDonald, by Sabu and Dick Powell, by Jack Lemmon and Tony Curtis, by Marilyn Monroe and Jane Russell. Now I wonder why. The older I get, the less I find entertainment entertaining.

# SECTION 4

# ART, ARCHITECTURE and CONSTRUCTION

There is no doubt that the change from humanity wandering as nomadic tribes and scavenging for food, to its present state of a rapidly expanding population, mostly crowded into cities, is the result of humanity discovering that crops could be grown and harvested, that animals could be husbanded and used for transport, milk and meat, and that people could live together peacefully in groups for mutual advantage. Permanent shelters were built and occupied. From this start civilisation grew and prospered. Humanity has produced great works of construction and art has flourished. What does the future hold?

# 36. MODERN ARCHITECTURE AND ART.

I hold the opinion that the conceiving, planning and construction of buildings, monuments, bridges, roads, dams and infrastructure systems are noble activities, and are among the great achievements of humanity. Without these creations civilisation would not have been possible. Of these different facets of construction the most inspirational can be architecture – although bridges and dams run a close second. Art is also an important facet of civilisation, being a product, as it is, of the instincts that have led to humanity becoming civilised.

It is inspirational to walk up to, enter and experience the great buildings of the past. It is not possible for anyone, with even the smallest degree of sensitivity, to approach and enter such diverse constructions as the temples at Thebes, the Egyptian pyramids or the massive statues at Abu Simbel, the Greek Parthenon, the Paraportiani of Mykonos, the remains of the Temple of Poseidon at Sounion (with Byron's name carved, by him, into a column base), the Pantheon or any other classic Roman building, the Hagia Sofia of Istanbul, Japan's Ise Shrine, or any Gothic cathedral, without them feeling pride that humans can construct such things.

I have had similar twinges of pride when looking at the Golden Gate Bridge, the Firth of Forth, Maillart's simple and sublime arched bridges and, more recently, the Lord Foster team's Millau Viaduct. I am impressed by great buildings and great constructions, although I sometimes wonder what has led to the huge effort being made in some cases.

I am similarly impressed by superb works of art. How Michelangelo released his elegant David from a block of inanimate marble is beyond me. David now stands in pride of place in Florence surrounded by awe-struck tourists. There are many other sculpted creations that have enchanted me – but most are from ages past. Paintings have also captured me. Da Vinci, Giotto, Botticelli, Titian, Caravaggio, Raphael, several of the impressionists, and Van Gogh have left me in admiring awe. I am not so smitten with many of the later, famous artists such as Klee and Kandinsky and I am particularly unimpressed by the later works of Pablo Picasso and regard him as a world class salesman, not as a world class artist.

*Picasso is a world renowned artist whose works sell for many millions. Am I alone in considering that this portrait is an ugly daub?*

Now I come to the present. We appear to be in an age when our leading architects and artists are in a quandary. Although they are equipped with tools that are superior to those wielded by the masters of the past, they appear to be unable to produce works that are better than, or as good as, the works of the ancient masters, or of the masters of the renaissance. This has resulted in leading architects producing twisted and messy buildings that do not fulfil their functions as they should, that are often ungainly and unnecessarily complicated, that lack grace and logic, that are extremely expensive, and that are very difficult to build and maintain. Our artists are similarly stressed, and only rarely produce works of the quality of the old masters. Instead, they often attempt to elicit shock, not admiration, and they succeed.

Even though they set out to shock, the latest outputs of some architects and artists are accepted and applauded by the critics. We appear to be living in an age when the critics are subservient to egotistical salespersons, who have incredible self-confidence, masquerading as architects and artists. Once buildings and works of art spoke for themselves. Now buildings require ridiculous explanations from their creators, and the critics and academics swallow whole the nonsense they produce. I now give you a couple of examples.

The first is Wolf D. Prix's explanation of his Confluence Museum. *"The building comprises an assortment of protruding elements all elevated over a public space. The composition of the structure combines a crystal and a cloud symbolising the known and the unknown, or the familiar environment of the present and the uncertain vagueness of the future. The cloud represents the largest part of the building and has been constructed to represent a spaceship stationed above the building. The crystal was designed to house the circulation space."* All this magnificent, if hard to comprehend, explanation for a building that is structurally extremely messy internally, that is extremely expensive, and that has not fulfilled its aim of quietly protecting and exhibiting artefacts to enlighten seekers of knowledge.

The second is Frank Gehry's discussion of his Louis Vuitton Foundation: *"It couldn't be a normal building. It had to be a park building. It had to be diaphanous and float"*. Mr. Gehry did not explain why a park building has to be diaphanous and float, and he and I obviously see things differently. I see the Foundation as a complicated mess of inappropriate and ungainly structural members and panels that are difficult (if not impossible) to clean, and will be a maintenance problem. Far from floating, many parts of the building appear to be in the process of falling over. Yet this ungainly and expensive mess has gained renown in architectural circles.

*Prix's Confluence Museum internally. Is this structural mess really a crystal or a cloud? Is it great – or even good – architecture? Where are the artefacts it is supposed to display? It is very expensive and it has been applauded by the critics, so it must be good.*

*Frank Gehry's Louis Vuitton – "diaphanous and floating" – Foundation. It is unusual, and difficult and expensive to build, but is it great architecture? Is it falling over? Will it be a maintenance nightmare?*

*Here we have a sample of Mr. Gehry's mixture of laminated timber and steel that comprises the structure of his Foundation. How does this compare in structural honesty and elegance with Gothic cathedrals? Does the fact that it is messily complicated make it good architecture? It was certainly difficult to build.*

In Australia we have the Perth Arena, which was adjudged the best building in Australia in 2014 by the Australian Institute of Architects, so it also must be good. It has been discussed by Mr. Howard Raggatt, one of its award winning architects, in the following terms. It is *"A large and exquisitely complex project of urban integration and patron experience."*

*Is this disorganised mess designed by Ashton, Raggatt and McDougall great architecture? Is it the proper setting for a sporting arena? What ever happened to elegance and form following function? And its basement car park leaks. Australia's best building for 2014?*

Should a sporting arena be exquisitely complex? The Romans apparently did not think so. And it certainly does not integrate into its urban surroundings. Mr. Raggatt has provided its inspiration, which was partly: *"the impossible twelve-sided Eternity Puzzle by the crazy Lord Monckton."*

Should a building be inspired by a puzzle or should it be inspired by its functions and its materials as Greek theatres were? The award winning building, Mr. Raggatt points out, *"remains puzzling, as if in a language no longer spoken"*. He further says that, *"No matter how cleverly juxtaposed, how mysteriously emblazoned, how boldly urbanist, how secretly transfigured the pieces were; no matter how gritty our contextualism was, how difficult our junctions or how elegant our surfaces; no matter how interconnected the spaces were, how spectacular their volumes or how many beautiful acoustic plywood panels, projected shadows or supergraphics they had,"* the puzzle remained. To my simple engineer's mind this is just sententious waffle. It is not the language of buildings. Is it possible that ARM are having a joke at the public's expense?

As both Prix and Gehry are considered to be at the forefront of their profession internationally, and as Ashton, Raggatt and McDougall are Gold Medal Award winners for their profession in Australia, I must be wrong in considering their overblown, structurally complex, difficult to build and extremely expensive concoctions silly, even inane, sculptures; not elegant, functional architecture.

The buildings of all are uncomfortable in appearance, difficult to navigate through, and have excessive circulation space. All use materials inappropriately. The awarded buildings, and the overblown writings that back them, might be considered to be sophistication by others, but I regard both as sophistry. As the profession generally, and the architectural award panels, and the architectural critics, applaud these buildings, I realise I am missing something, but I will continue to be critical of them. Despite the public backing of their efforts by the architectural critics, the elite of the architectural profession and its applauding academics, I find I am not alone. I have yet to have had a practising architect tell me that these buildings are great architecture and that I am wrong, and why I am wrong. Is the emperor wearing elegant clothes?

I can understand why Bernard Arnault of Louis Vuitton, France's richest man, selected Gehry to design his Foundation. Gehry is the architect du jour, and it is a well-established fact that riches do not necessarily coincide with taste, so if M. Arnault wished to make a splash he could not have done better than commission Mr. Gehry. While I understand that, I do not understand why independent critics have so often lauded the building and have not pointed out its many shortcomings. For instance its exhibition spaces total 3,850 sq.m and its total area is some 11,000 sq.m. This seems to be an excessive amount of circulation space for a building that has as its reason for being the housing works of art. I can forgive a lack of functionality in works of art, but not in buildings. Why have critics so readily accepted Gehry's misshapen and expensive nonsenses, with their ignoring of efficient structural mechanics, their wasteful use of materials, their maintenance problems, and their poor responses to their functional requirements? A building's first duty is to provide protection for its contents and those who inhabit it. A building should not be a flowery output of an over-heated imagination, powered by incredible self-assurance. Being handsome or beautiful and adding to its surroundings is also a duty of a building, but its first duty is to act functionally. I regard the Louis Vuitton Foundation as an expensive and poorly functioning piece of sculpture that will deteriorate.

*Jean Nouvel's Paris Philharmonic Hall. Is this balanced elegance? Does its exterior reflect its functions or its necessary structural skeleton? Is it a maintenance nightmare? It certainly badly overran its budget.*

How did architecture get to a state in which unbalanced, ridiculously difficult to build and hugely expensive buildings such as the Louis Vuitton Foundation, Jean Nouvel's ugly and ill-balanced Paris Philharmonic Hall, and Gehry's Walt Disney Concert Hall, with its ridiculous shambles of curved shapes, are regarded as the epitome of great architecture? It is the responsibility of architectural critics and architectural academics to critically examine what is built and provide balanced comment for us lesser mortals. Are they fulfilling this responsibility? Is it that we are going through a period of the Emperor's new clothes? I hope this phase of stupid excess passes and we return to a period in which architecture that is functional, logical, balanced, graceful (even elegant) and ages well is, again, the preferred architecture.

I realise that logic and art do not necessarily go together and that beauty is in the eye of the beholder, as is so often quoted, so I know that my opinions of Pablo Picasso's daub the *"Woman in Fur Hat and Collar"*, and of Gehry's applauded buildings will not be widely agreed with, and that many will still publically admire the works of Nouvel, Wolf D. Prix and other architects, such as Ashton, Raggatt and McDougal, who appear to be driven by a wish to be different, but I have to say that Picasso's green faced woman with fat and ugly green hands and a misshapen hat is not my idea of great art. It is also poorly painted but I suppose it has the virtue of being different, which is probably what Picasso was aiming at.

What the world needs is critics who understand the problems, possibilities and trials of art and architecture, who look at what is produced in a balanced manner, and who do not succumb to the latest way out fashion; critics who analyse and report honourably and are not sycophants of the latest fashionable genius, and critics who report their findings in language that is understandable.

## 37. IS THERE A PLACE FOR PLAYFULNESS IN ARCHITECTURE?

The answer is an obvious "yes" but, in my view, it should be confined to circuses, Luna Parks and showgrounds. In the general field of construction, and I consider construction to be the foundation of civilization, I believe there is little place for playfulness, but there is certainly room for structural imagination and decoration. For structural imagination I look to the works of Frei Otto, Pier Luigi Nervi, Felix Candela, Fazlur Khan and Kenzo Tange – not to Gehry, Hadid, Nouvel and their followers – especially not to Gehry's sculptures. For decoration I applaud the highly decorated buildings of Antoni Gaudi, the wonderful, glowing tile patterns on so many Moslem mosques and schools, some colourful Chinese edifices and the carved timbers on Japanese shrines and temples. Although I have some reservations about them, imagine the loss if the domes of Saint Basil's in Moscow or the Florence Cathedral did not have their colours.

Structural imagination and the application of colour should be thoughtful, not playful. To achieve great architecture taste, proportion, sound structural approaches and elegant use of materials must be amalgamated skillfully. Great architecture comes from innate artistry, technical skill, understanding of the potentialities of materials and effort. It is not achieved from playing architectural games, however attractive that might be to some.

In my view architecture should not be a contest between the most messily jointed, complex and difficult to build structures, such as those the current doyen of sculptural architects, Frank Gehry, has managed to produce for the Louis Vuitton Foundation. This building, applauded by the critics, uses incompatible, rare and expensive materials and complex layouts so that the building is inefficiently planned, costs more than is reasonable, and will probably be a nightmare to maintain. It compares with Nouvel's Paris Philharmonic Concert Hall in these regards. Such buildings rank, in terms of architecture, with how Warhol's banal Campbell's Soup Cans painting ranks with true art, in my opinion.

Buildings must first meet the practical demands for which they have been constructed. They should be designed in a manner that makes clear how they are to be built, and they should generally be built from materials that are reasonably available, compatible and that can be readily maintained. They should, also, enhance their surroundings.

Although I put meeting the practical demands of buildings first, there are other, more subtle, demands on design architects. Some buildings need to create an atmosphere, an ambience that transcends practicality. Religious buildings – some cathedrals, mosques and synagogues and even Stonehenge come to mind. University buildings should not only provide space, but should also provide inspiration. The university city of Cambridge is an example. Architecture is a complex human activity. It requires practitioners who are conscientious, have a store of practical knowledge, innately understand the capabilities of the materials with which they are working, and who also understand the construction process. Architecture is both an artistic challenge and a practical challenge. It requires imagination, understanding of structural actions, appreciation of proportion, ability to design for elegance, an understanding of what is required to provide both a suitable ambience and the practicalities of a building – light, climate control, circulation, maintenance and the frameworks necessary to provide communications, power, water and effluent disposal. Good architecture should be detailed in such a manner that it will age gracefully. There is little room for playfulness unless that is a requirement of the client. There is, however, room for decoration.

Good architects are well aware of all this, of course, but these basic tenets are often being ignored by architects who now follow, or create, fashions. It seems to me that architecture has become a victim of a series of fashions that have spread throughout the world, even though they are quite inappropriate.

Those architects who have abandoned taste, proportion, elegance, practicality and tradition in favour of strangely sculptured shapes, produce architecture that is difficult to build, is extremely expensive and is difficult to maintain. This impractical architecture is now given awards by assessing panels. If the Perth Arena was the best building in Australia in 2014, I despair - and the basement leaks.

I realize that, as a structural engineer, my views on architecture will not be taken too seriously by the profession, but I have been encouraged by the positive comments of several senior architects who have read my short book *"Egotecture?"* Although I am not an architect I have worked closely with some fine architects both in Australia and overseas on award winning and leading edge buildings. I have the advantage of being able to stand back from, and not having to compete with, other architects.

## 38. GREAT ARCHITECTURE.

A question that I have often pondered is – what makes great architecture? If you have read *"Architecture of the Absurd"* by John Silber, and agree with its theme, as I do, or my book *"Egotecture?"*, you will know why I am far from enchanted with much of what is highly thought of and applauded, as cutting edge architecture today, and that I am less than impressed with many of the undisciplined award winners that are written about in glowing, if difficult to interpret, terms by critics and academics.

In *"Egotecture?"* I discussed buildings my wife Kaye and I had visited during a tour of Europe in 2015, organised by the planner Jim Webber and the architect Malcolm Carver. I found much to be admired, but I have been critical of several buildings in both Australia and overseas – buildings that have been given awards, and that now occupy a high place in the architectural pantheon. Several buildings I have criticised have been the work of today's architectural heroes and heroines – Safdie, Calatrava, Libeskind, Nouvel, Coop Himmelb(l)au, Hadid, Ashton Raggatt and McDougal, and Gehry.

Reactions to *"Egotecture?"* have been interesting. I have yet to get considered and balanced negative criticisms of the positions I have taken in discussing the buildings being produced by these highly thought of, and awarded architects, or even any minor disagreements from members of the profession, or from architectural academia. I have had several respected practising architects agree with me. If I am right, why is the profession giving awards where it is giving them? One criticism I received from my sons, and others, I have taken to heart. It is that while I have been free with my opinions I have not provided a basis for deciding what makes great architecture great. I will now outline what I consider to be the qualities great architecture needs. Before I do, I make it clear that I fully recognise that the act of creation is very difficult, and that the act of criticism is relatively easy. I also recognise that tastes vary, and what one person considers to be a building of quality another can consider to be badly flawed. So there is unlikely to be universal agreement as to what constitutes great, or even good, architecture.

What follows are my views, formed after many years of consideration and involvement in design and construction processes, and why I have formed the views I have. It was, I believe, Vitruvius, the Roman architect, who propounded a basis for good architecture in the 1$^{st}$ century AD. It is a basis with which I agree, but it needs updating. He said a good building should satisfy the principles of *firmitas, utilitas* and *venustas*. This was originally translated as *firmness, commodity* and *delight.* Today I think that this might be more readily translated as *soundness, practicality, longevity, cost effectiveness, compliance with structural principles* and *beauty.*

- *Soundness.* To be great, or even good, architecture must provide permanent and adequate shelter, and protection, for what it houses. It must be robust enough to withstand the loadings to which it will be exposed, and control internal conditions of light, ventilation, climate and acoustics – it must provide a satisfactory ambience – and, where necessary, communication, safety; circulation routes and the practicalities of plumbing and security. Unless a building is sound and provides for these things it is not good, let alone great, architecture in my opinion.
- *Practicality.* For architecture to be good it must be practical and have an honesty of purpose. It should be efficiently planned, have understandable circulation routes, be designed to be reasonably

buildable, be built from materials that are appropriate for the period of its construction, the climate in which is set, and the skills and equipment that are reasonably available. It can be leading edge but it should not be too *outré*.
- *Longevity*. Good architecture is designed and built to last, without excessive maintenance, unless it is designed for constant refreshment as the Ise Shrine of Japan is. This Shinto Shrine is re-built every 20 years and is the exception. Most good architecture should have a life that is as trouble free as possible.
- *Cost effectiveness*. Good architecture should not be wastefully extravagant. This does not mean it must be cheap, or that it should not have an advanced structure or enhancing decorations. (Consider the losses if gothic cathedrals did not have their fluted vaults, Gaudi's architecture did not have its decorations, and the peaked shells of the Sydney Opera House did not grace Bennelong Point). It does mean that it should not be wastefully overblown to meet some fashion with the object of showing off, or creating a stir.
- *Compliance with structural principles*. This could be considered to be only a structural engineer's concern, but I believe that unless those using a building can see that it is structurally right – and I believe most people have a sense for structural rigour – they are not comfortable with a building. This is currently a vexed area because architects, and their structural advisors, are now able to produce distorted structures, by courtesy of the analytical powers of modern computer programs, and are doing so to show how up to date they are. Structural discipline does not have to be obeyed as it has in the past. Whilst admiring the abilities that have to be employed to design and construct distorted structures, I do not consider that the lack of discipline displayed by such structures is good architecture. I realize that I could be accused of hypocrisy because I have been laudatory about peaked gothic arches with their requirement for flying buttresses, and I have been particularly admiring of Gaudi's works, when both could be accused of lacking structural discipline, and unnecessary cost. My defence is

that the gothic arches were developed by trial and error and Gaudi, the great Gaudi, arrived at his structures with three dimensional models, so his structures are basically right. I consider that clever but distorted structures do not produce great, or even good, architecture any more than tricks on one-wheeled bicycles in circuses produce great art.

- *Beauty.* There are few rules as to what is beautiful. Beauty is a combination of qualities that please the senses of individuals – and that is highly personal. What is considered to be beautiful is a combination of the sensitivities with which an individual is born, and that individual's education and upbringing. In architecture, beauty is considered to be a function of the qualities, colours, textures and finishes of the construction materials from which a building is made, the disposition of those materials and their shapes, the proportions of the elements and the spaces enclosed, and – to my limited engineer's mind – the integrity, the truthfulness, of the structures of a building's parts. License can be taken with proportion (are the proportions of the Taj Mahal ideal?) and with structural integrity (are the domes of St. Basil's cathedral in Red Square structurally ideal?), and the buildings can still be regarded highly. Would they be even better had both been structurally truthful and of ideal proportions?

These rules of Vitruvius, and my assumptions as to their wider meanings, do not apply only to architecturally designed buildings in my opinion. They should also apply to many machines, highways, pathways, bridges, towers, dams and protection walls.

As an engineer, I realise that my views are unlikely to be sought after by the Frank Gehrys, the Daniel Libeskinds, the Jean Nouvels and the Wolf D. Prixs of this world, or by those who follow in their expensive and overwrought paths, but I have recorded them anyway and now wait to be told how I am wrong, and why I am wrong, by those more knowledgeable. How anyone can consider that the unbelievable mess that the self-satisfied Frank Gehry has concocted for the LUMA building in Arles is good, let alone great, architecture, and that it complements such a benign setting as that beautiful town, is completely beyond me. It is, as many of Gehry's buildings are, an ill disciplined, twisted and distorted sculpture. Only time will tell if it functions as it should.

The first requirement of great architecture is, surely, that it fulfils its reason for having been built. It should efficiently protect that which it houses, and it must provide an environment that nurtures its contents, whatever they are. Unless a building does this, it has not fulfilled its primary duty. Other requirements are that it is built in a manner, and from materials, that will last for the period for which it has been built, and should not require excessive maintenance and cleaning. Great architecture should be planned in a manner that will allow its protected contents to circulate within it efficiently, be they people, machines, books, works of art, or services of various types. It should naturally provide climate control and lighting, and efficiently provide these artificially, if necessary. It absolutely must be able to bear the loads of any traffic, and the forces of nature to which it will be subjected, without undue distortion – it must be structurally competent. I realise that these are all practical issues – issues of planning, material selection and of various engineering disciplines – but unless these practical requirements are met, the building produced might be imposing, it might be an interesting piece of sculpture, it might be a flight of fancy, but it will not be a piece of great architecture.

However, there are factors that distinguish great architecture from competent architecture, that distinguish the artistic from the mundane – scale, proportion, massing, the quality of surfaces, harmony of materials, honesty of purpose, structural integrity, the quality and elegance of detailing, colour, and the value of the spaces enclosed. These are the artistic elements of a construction that separate great architecture from competent architecture, and there are, as yet, no hard and fast rules. Buildings some find to be artistically uplifting others can find to be gaudily overplayed messes. For several reasons I find Gehry's moulded metal shapes and shiny surfaces, his distorted brickwork and columns at strange angles, and his badly detailed structures of disparate materials at random angles, to be irritating and not good, let alone great, architecture. No poetry emanates from them for me.

On the other hand I greatly admire Gaudi's ornate creations, possibly because of their structural integrity. I do not know why I admire Gothic cathedrals, and consider them to be great creations of humanity, but fail to find the satisfaction in them I find in the Cycladic architecture of Greece, in the wonderful shrines and temples of Japan, in the best of the classic Greek and Roman buildings, and in the stately splendour of some of France's chateaux. Perhaps it is because the Gothic cathedrals were deliberately conceived to overawe. I am mystified as to why the critics have so loudly sung the praises of Wolf D. Prix's Confluence Museum, and regard it as an architectural masterpiece, when I regard it as a ridiculously inelegant shambles that does not fulfil its role of displaying its objects to their best advantage, and is structurally wasteful. It appears to be a case of its designer allowing himself to be carried away with the possibilities of advanced computer abilities, and forgetting that discipline is necessary in all things. I also do not know why I so much admire the stately elegance of classic Greek and Roman temples, the facades and columns of Thebes and Abu Simbel, the complexities of Vlad's castle in Transylvania and of Japanese castles, when I am appalled by Nouvel's unbalanced Paris Philharmonic Hall.

I conclude by saying that there may not be simple rules as to what constitutes great architecture, but I repeat that even great architecture needs to obey the basic rules of function, climate control, reasonable longevity, and structural integrity and stability. It is nonsense to say that *"If a roof doesn't leak the architect has not been creative enough"* as the great Frank Lloyd Wright has been reported as saying. That which constitutes great architecture is what each of us finds is functionally and artistically satisfying. Our findings are probably coloured by what we have been taught, by what our contemporaries find to be great, and by the remains of glorious buildings from the past that are regarded as icons. And I am afraid that, although there will be loud disagreements, architecture is subject to the pronouncements of gurus and, worse, to fashion. What is considered to be great architecture in one period of history can be seen as soulless or even banal in another, and what can be considered as uninspiring simplicity in a period can be seen as beautifully proportioned and functional in another.

Issues and Challenges

Now I give you examples of buildings and some comments on them. Please make up your own minds as to which of them, if any, meets your criteria of great architecture.

*Part of the roof of the Hagia Sofia in Istanbul. This honest and imposing structure was built in the 5th century AD as a place of Christian worship. It is my view that it complies with the principles outlined by Vitruvius and that it is a great and peaceful architectural accomplishment.*

*This is part of the acclaimed Guggenheim Museum in Bilbao, Spain that was built only a few years ago. It is highly thought of in architectural circles. I find it clumsy, ill proportioned and ugly. In my view it does not comply with the Vitruvius principles.*

*This is an entrance to the famed and lauded Guggenheim Museum. I found this incredibly messy and that it does not meet Vitruvius's principles but it is generally highly praised by the architectural profession. Why?*

*The ceiling of the Sagrada Familia, Gaudi's final masterpiece, is intricately and serenely beautiful. In my view the building excels and meets Vitruvius's demands although there are places externally where I do not like his decoration.*

*Compare this ungainly mess, the Confluence Museum, designed by Coop Himmelb(l)au, with Gaudi's elegance. It is as bad, or even worse, internally and it is poorly laid out for a home that has the task of displaying artefacts. It would have been a nightmare to build. Where is the grace?*

*The Pont du Gard was built by the Romans. It is utilitarian, has lasted and fulfils its functional requirements. Vitruvius would have been impressed.*

*Another modern masterpiece, the Paris Philharmonic Concert Hall designed by Jean Nouvel. Unfortunately he fell out with the client over the cost. This does not meet the requirements of Vitruvius in my opinion. Do you find it graceful and elegant?*

*The incredibly elegant and practical Millau Viaduct produced by a team of which Lord Norman Foster was a part. It certainly complies with the requirements of Vitruvius. It not only does that – it is paying for itself.*

Issues and Challenges

*Perth Arena was designed by the Gold Medal winners ARM which means it must be Australian architecture at its best. It has a family resemblance to the Confluence Museum. I find it difficult to understand the 'commodity' provided by the pipe structure shown and why it is so badly distorted. Would Vitruvius have approved? Would Louis Sullivan? Would Frank Lloyd Wright? Would Louis Kahn?*

Once humankind settled into hubs, and civilised groups began to accumulate, 'permanent' buildings came into being. They have become the hallmark of civilisations. There have been periods of incredible accomplishments – the pyramids and temples of Egypt and the Aztecs, the Grecian and Roman explosions of growth and development, the wonderful buildings of the Arab civilisation that extended across northern Africa and southern Europe, the temples and shrines of the Orient, the many colourful buildings of India and the Middle East, the Gothic cathedrals that dot Europe and, more recently, the sky scrapers that the energetic USA has built. Currently we are seeing the unprecedented growth of major cities along the barren edges of the Persian Gulf; developments fuelled by oil riches. Where to now?

Humankind is obliged to awaken to the fact that we live on a finite globe, and we have no alternative but to protect its productive capacities. We have to limit our growth so we do not exceed those capacities. We should be aware that we have to live in peace and in balance with nature or we will likely destroy our world and ourselves.

How will humankind respond to these pressures, and how will we build for, and in, the future? What will we need to do to house our burgeoning generations? Will we build ever bigger ant hills with people living remotely from the ground as foreseen by Arthur C. Clarke? Will some of us become troglodytes and live underground as suggested by H. G. Wells? Will buildings become not only dwellings and work places but areas of plant and food production?

Where will architecture go? I hope it does not go further into the world of distortion.

## 39. THE FUTURE OF ARCHITECTURE AND CONSTRUCTION.

In the past there have been limitations on what can be built. Limitations were imposed by the materials available, the construction tools, equipment and skills, the means of documentation, the abilities to analyse complex structures, and the imagination and abilities of the designers that were then designing. Despite these limitations there have been periods during which humanity has produced some amazing and wonderful constructions, many of which leave us awestruck today.

Some examples are the pyramids and the statues and temples of ancient Egypt. How the Egyptians built the pyramids, and erected some of their huge statues, given the mechanical tools of the time is still in contention today. (See publications by Davidovits and others). Other wonders are the classic buildings of Greece and Rome, the complex and elegant pagodas and palaces of eastern Asia, the graceful wonders of the Gothic cathedrals of Europe, and the 16th century, and later, palaces and villas designed by Andrea Palladio, and others, with their lovely proportions and details.

Then the Industrial Revolution developed in the late 18th century. Steam was harnessed and inventions such as Hargreaves' Spinning Jenny changed the manner in which things were made forever. Powered machinery led to factories and mass production. Steam powered transportations on both land and sea were developed. The means of producing iron economically was conceived by Bessemer. Then in the 1840s Portland cement, as we know it, was developed. Today our primary building materials are still concrete made from aggregates and Portland cement, and steel, although other metals are called on and terra cotta and timber is still widely used.

Into this world of new materials and powered machinery came architects who used them. Louis Sullivan, Daniel Burnham, Mies van der Rohe, Frank Lloyd Wright, Walter Gropius, William Van Alen, Shreve, Lamb and Harmon, Le Corbusier, Louis Kahn, Oscar Niemeyer and, more recently, Skidmore, Owings and Merrill, Lord Norman Foster, Joern Utzon, Kenzo Tange, I. M. Pei and Renzo Piano, to name a few. The works of these designers have used these basic materials and the construction equipment available skilfully, although not always to my personal taste, or in accordance with what I consider to be best principles. Their works have been based on practical use of materials and construction techniques and equipment available – cranes, concrete pumps, scaffolding and formwork systems, and people moving systems – and their designs have been made possible by the abilities of their structural engineers. (What would Utzon have done with his opera house's peaked, nesting arches if Ove Arup's engineers had not arrived at their solution? What would FLW have been able to do without JJ Polivka or Tange without Yoshikatsu Tsuboi?). As structural analysis techniques have developed there has been a parallel development in mechanical, electrical and electronic systems that are more efficient, and less energy consuming, and that control light, internal climate conditions, safety and security. Building at this time has much to admire. But is it all good and where is it heading?

Now architectural designers are searching for new and innovative approaches, To be able to use these recent approaches they can – and do – ignore the lessons of the past and they appear to often ignore what I regard as fundamentals – cost effectiveness, buildability, efficiency of circulation and operation, the requirement for minimising maintenance, and providing a trouble free life span.

Now the world has a new group of designers who, because they can, stretch their buildings to design limits. This group includes Frank Gehry,

Daniel Libeskind, Zaha Hadid, Santiago Calatrava, Ashton Raggatt and Mc Dougal, Koop Himmelb(l)au and Jean Nouvel. These 'iconic' architects appear to be intent on creating free form sculptural objects. Form no longer follows function. Buildings are expensively twisted for no good reason – just at the designer's whim. Claddings are shaped to sculptural forms, not to functional requirements. Structures are deliberately made three dimensionally messy and difficult to build. Graceful proportions are sacrificed for what designers consider to be bold statements, and critics and academics applaud them.

Why have designers and critics abandoned the tenets of form following function, of proportions being paramount, and of structures being practical and basically elegant, as they once did for important buildings? In disparate civilisations cathedrals, mosques, shrines, synagogues, temples and important public buildings were once built that met these requirements. Now the aim of designers appears to be to astound, not to please. Once the most overwrought and over decorated of Rococo buildings still obeyed the basic laws that are now ignored by the architectural geniuses of today. Why has there been this change?

Is it because architects are suffering from a syndrome that is also affecting today's painters and sculptors – the problem that they cannot equal, let alone better, the works of the masters of the past, so they produce works that are inferior and distorted, with the aim of shocking? My questions are – do Picasso's distorted portraits of women compare with Rembrandt's portraits or Andy Warhol's Campbell's Soup Cans compare with works by Michelangelo? Do Gehry's and Nouvel's unbalanced sculptures better the designs of ancient Rome or of Kahn, Tange and Niemeyer?

If the problem for architectural designers is that they cannot better the works of the past, as I consider it probably is, and they need to search for new paths to follow, will they continue to follow the route of distorted structures, shapes that are sculptured for no good reason, huge cantilevers that provide no protection from sun, wind or rain but are expensive, fashionably growing plants on inappropriate surfaces, using timber externally when it is a material that needs constant attention, using clay bricks and laminated timber inappropriately, as Gehry does, and worrying more about sycophantic acceptance by the tame architectural critics than about how well their buildings function, how cost effective they are, and how they will weather in the climatic conditions to which they will be subjected.

So – where to in the future? Further down the present course of freehand sculptures, that was probably started by Mendelsohn with his Einstein Tower of 1921, and given impetus by Le Corbusier with his Ronchamp Chapel of 1955 (that is not aging well), and is now starring Frank Gehry's bent and twisted wonders, and such clumsy blots as Jean Nouvel's Paris Philharmonic Hall? Or will there be a return to designers designing for appropriate use of building materials, proportion of surfaces and spaces, efficient climate control, permanent weather proofing (great architecture no longer needs to leak), usable space and efficient circulation?

I do not know, but I am not confident that the construction world will soon enter into another golden age of architecture – of elegant and practical buildings – an age that will be admired by future generations, and respected, as so many buildings, bridges, and transport systems with their supporting buildings from the past are respected today.

## 40. CONSTRUCTION.

Is construction in Australia the competitive industry it is supposed to be? Is the process of selecting designers, contractors, sub-contractors and suppliers on the basis of what each says its cost will be, the usual system today, the best selection medium? Does this selection on cost produce optimum answers? Does it build teamwork? Does it produce an environment in which those involved strive for optimum finished products? Or does it produce an environment in which each party is encouraged to work to minimise its input, and its responsibilities, so that it can remain commercially sustainable and avoid legal action being taken against it? Does it create a construction industry in which those who perform ethically, and to the best of their abilities, suffer financially?

It is my view that the process of selection of those given the responsibility of creating a new edifice – the designers, the constructors, the suppliers and the sub-contractors – on price is fatally flawed. It often leads to the design and construction teams acting as warring parties, with each entity trying to protect its own interests, instead of working as a team to produce products that are useful to clients and the public, as cost effectively as possible, with high standards of finish. And it often results in cost overruns and expensive litigations in courts that, sometimes, do not truly understand the complications of construction.

No sensible client or leader assembling a team, to undertake any other activity than construction, would consider for a moment selecting team members because they were the lowest cost players available. Selecting any part of the construction team on price – the designers, the head contractors, sub-contractors and suppliers – is a recipe for problems and for costs that are real, but that do not show up as building costs. They include waste executive time when problems arise, the cost of the experts who inevitably get dragged in, the costs of their investigations, and the high costs of the legal fraternity who become involved as the disagreements escalate. However, despite its obvious flaws, selection on cost is the system most now adopt. It is not the optimum system, in my opinion. Are there other and better possibilities?

There certainly are those who consider that the present system is the optimum system, and there are those who consider that a system of selection on merit, past performance and the skills and experience of those who will be involved is open to corruption. There are also those who believe that documentation – contracts, drawings and specifications – can be produced that lay down what is to be done, how it is to be done and in a set time frame, with clarity and unambiguously, so that there will be no basis for future disagreements. My experience is that documents are never perfect, especially when design fees have been cut to a minimum. There are always areas where issues are cloudy, where instructions can be read in more than one way, and where standards set are not crystal clear and can be read in a way that is different to their intended meaning. There is also the temptation for the designers to over-specify so that they have a margin for error – a built in factor of safety.

When teams are assembled on the basis of merit, not cost, and are reasonably led and reasonably rewarded, as problems arise, as document shortcomings come to light, or as construction mistakes occur, they can be dealt with quickly and fairly by the team.

There are other major advantages in assembling a full team, including those who will construct what is being designed, at the beginning of a project. These advantages include that the designers get the benefit of expert construction advice as they design and document and both the designers and the constructors then become responsible for the working documents, so that the constructors have a sense of authorship of the documents and will try to overcome difficulties if there are shortcomings, instead of searching for flaws that can be exploited for a monetary gain. The constructors can advise on the best way of doing things for economy and quality. Team spirit arises, and disagreements are reduced. When my practice has been part of a total team at the beginning of a project, the result has always been excellent. I believe the reason has been that the team spirit that prevails has all parts working towards a common end – a good and economical result.

My preferred team approach is for the members of the design team and the head contractor to be selected on their track records and the personnel that will be seconded to the project. The selected head contractor has the tasks of preparing a construction schedule, calling the sub-contracts, arranging for the necessary supplies, arranging payments in conjunction with the QS (the quantity surveyor) and overseeing the quality of the works. Sub-contract and supply packages are called and let as they are needed. They are not necessarily let to the lowest bidders but are selected on the basis of quality and value, decided by the client representative, the head contractor, the QS, the designer of the element being decided and the project manager. Though there is a cost I consider that all members of the design team should be retained throughout the contract period, and paid to superintend the elements they have designed. Should any member of the design team, or any sub-contractor or supplier, not demonstrate its commitment to the project or not meet expectations they will not be asked to continue their involvement, or will not be required to provide further tenders for packages as they are let. As work progresses the costs are carefully monitored by the head contractor and the QS. When projects have been built using this system they have been successful, the quality has been excellent, they have been finished on time, they have produced value for money and it has been possible for the client to make modifications as work progresses without there being high costs for 'extras'.

There are certainly beneficiaries of the present system. Because those involved have been selected on the basis of cost, because they have to attempt to cut corners to avoid losing money, because there is little or no team spirit, and because each party is looking after its own self-interests, disagreements between those involved are almost inevitable. Designers, with the best will in the world, have to limit their input, and cannot afford to examine alternative possibilities or to document as thoroughly as they might otherwise do. There is a strong temptation for designers to overdesign, to ensure they are not caught wanting. To save their costs and to meet their limited budgets, head contractors can be tempted to employ lower quality and less expensive staff, and to limit the time they spend on site so that they do not adequately control the quality and progress of their sub-contractors – who were selected on the basis of a low price – as they would if they were better rewarded. Arguments develop over the quality of materials being provided by suppliers, who were also selected on the basis of a low price, and sub-contractors find flaws in documents they can exploit to boost their take on a tender figure that was too low.

War can commence, often with polite smiles and clenched teeth. From what then becomes a roiling mess, benefits arise for 'experts' and legal practitioners. Both these groups much prefer to be on the side that wins, so both try to find the positives of their client's position, and as many flaws in the opposition's position as they can. Their drive is not to settle fairly but to win. There is no real pressure on either group to find simple solutions to disputes and to settle them as quickly and as amicably as possible. The longer an argument drags on, the greater the fees for those doing the arguing.

The adversarial system that serves so well in most legal cases is not suited to settling building disputes as fairly, as economically and as quickly as possible. It can arrive at the wrong answers because the lawyers arguing the case, and the judges deciding where responsibilities lie, do not have a complete understanding of the complexities of the problems about which they are arguing and deciding. They can be led astray by clever and glib experts who, instead of taking a disinterested stance, as they should, become advocates and attempt to sway the court in which they are appearing. Not all experts are equal, and some, very technically able people, are not able to express themselves well under pressure, especially about complex technical matters, whereas some less knowledgeable experts can present what is actually doubtful evidence with confidence and aplomb. Personality can sway judges.

There is another group that benefits from the present system – unscrupulous head contractors. They can benefit in a number of ways. Having won a tender, they can attempt to make a profit by shopping for lower prices from sub-contractors and suppliers. Anxious to maintain their businesses, sub-contractors and suppliers can be coerced into lowering their tendered price, sometimes by lowering the quality of their input to the project. This can lead to arguments, and become another thorn in the side of good relations on the site. Another possible tactic is for a contractor to load the prices charged for the early trades and activities so that early payments are greater than costs. This means that the contractor is operating with a positive cash flow. If all goes well, and the project is completed to the satisfaction of the client, this tactic is of limited value, but if problems arise that result in the termination of the contract, the head contractor can walk away and still be financially in front.

Another means by which head contractors can benefit themselves is by holding money on sub-contractors and suppliers. This provides liquidity for the contractor at the cost of others. There are controls for this, but no sub-contractor or supplier wants to offend a major contractor, so it is still practised. And the last card a head contractor can play, and it has been known that contractors play it more than once, is for a contractor to declare itself bankrupt after having paid its executives and its owner's handsome salaries and dividends. A constructing firm can go broke, but the owners can continue to live extremely comfortably, and they can even start another operation. Those sub-contractors and suppliers building the construction, and those for whom it is being built, suffer financially. In my view selection of the design and construction teams on the basis of price is very flawed.

I know of sound contractors with skills, good staff and good track records who have given up contracting rather than continuing to try to compete in the world of selection on price.

There is no perfect answer to what is the complicated problem of arriving at systems to handle building disputes. My own view is that to reduce their frequency, the system of selection of the team members – the designers, the contractors, the sub-contractors and the suppliers – has to be changed. If teams are assembled on the basis of compatibility and previous performance, and paid reasonably, instead of having to fight for a fair reward, most of the present problems would evaporate, leaving 'experts', one of which I have been, with a good deal less to do.

Either the team can be selected on the basis of ability and fees agreed or, if that is not acceptable, perhaps it would be preferable to go to tender with a short list of honourable tenderers and to then choose the tenderer who is closest to the mean of the figures tendered. The advantages of the first alternative is that the whole team is in place when the designs are being finalised, so that the builders can act in an advisory capacity and team spirit is more likely to develop. The advantage of the second is that the cost is more likely to be the right cost than the figure tendered by the lowest tenderer.

The building industry in Australia has drifted into what I regard as an unfortunate, cost driven system that is now accepted as reasonable and normal. This, in my opinion, is wrong. Instead, the industry should be looking for a system that is not adversarial, a system that is a team game. We in the building industry should be spending less time, mental and physical energy, and waste cost, on arguments between the various groups, and more on arriving at systems that promote teamwork, and then demonstrating to clients that our new systems actually produce better results for them and for society.

Putting together teams of like-minded and ethical designers, contractors and suppliers can lower total costs because it lowers the costs of arguments and litigation, it is more likely to result in economical designs, and it will help overcome another deep-seated shortcoming of the construction industry – the problem of some parts of the industry taking more than a fair share of the financial pie, without performing to a level that justifies their rewards. Owners of private construction companies, and executives of public companies can reward themselves excessively, and do so. This leads to those actually carrying out the work also demanding high remunerations and getting them, because they have the industrial muscle to force the society in which they live to reward them highly.

The result of this spiral is that Australia has become an expensive place in which to build or manufacture, even though the team parts are selected on the basis of cost. Because parts of the building industry are under the control of unscrupulous people and unions, our global competitiveness is falling. Too many of those involved in construction place their highest priorities on maximum reward for minimum effort, instead of attempting to earn more than they are paid. Who has not seen groups standing around in their high-vis jackets and their hard hats, on construction sites, guarded over by others with Stop/Slow signs, watching a crane or a low loader or talking in groups? This is not what currently happens in the energetic and burgeoning societies such as South Korea and China. There, those on site, or those who are engaged in factories, work with energy so that their production costs are low.

The ethos of less work/more money prevalent in the Australian building industry is not yet universal, but it is growing. The trend must be reversed so that our industries, including our building industry, can remain competitive. So far Australia has been able to sustain a high standard of living because of the efforts of previous generations, and by its primary production of food and its mining, but these use only a small, and shrinking, percentage of the working population. For the long term success of our society it is necessary that we all compete on the world market in all we do, and that includes construction.

# 41. SETTLING CONSTRUCTION DISPUTES.

The following opinions are those of a person who has spent most of his life working as a consulting structural engineer, and who has concluded that the construction industry is not well served by the systems by which disputes are currently being settled.

I have seen disputes arise out of differing interpretations of contract documents, due to accidents and structural failures, because of disagreements about the quality of materials, finishes and construction standards, and about costs. In the early part of my career these were settled in discussions between client representatives, contractors and suppliers, quantity surveyors and design team members. Now they are settled in expensive, fully fledged legal battles in courts. Earlier on the client/design team had meetings with the construction team at which agreements were reached, albeit sometimes with ill grace. Now we have teams of battling and disinterested lawyers and experts outdoing each other. The aim of each team is to win – not to arrive at reasonable settlements.

In the early years of my career the major clients were the State and Commonwealth governments with their requirements for schools, hospitals, university buildings, roads, bridges, railways, distribution systems, housing and gaols. The Governments had various departments for each of these areas led by people who were long serving and honourable. They were interested in serving Australia well and the politicians of the day listened to them. Much of the W.A. State government's works were carried out by day labour organizations who worked closely with the designers, but changes were occurring.

Encouraged by the Brand/Court governments industries began to set up in the State. A refinery was built at Kwinana. It became the centrepiece for an industrial area. Kewdale and Osborne Park started to blossom as areas where things were made. Earlier a new State Brickworks was built at Armadale and later Ric' New started his Midland Brickworks using the latest clay brick making technology. Private industry was growing as the population grew.

The construction industry was also changing. Builders who had directly employed teams of carpenters, labourers, bricklayers and concreters were replaced by tight knit groups of organizers who employed sub-contractors, and bargained with suppliers. Several of the traditional builders retired from active involvement. Contracting became much more a matter of arranging inputs from the various parties that needed to be involved, and overseeing the quality and progress of the work than of actually laying bricks and pouring concrete. Builders became organizers with small offices who owned little equipment.

Another innovation was the arrival of independent quantity surveyors who produced Bills of Quantities that enabled builders, sub-contractors and suppliers to price accurately. Prior to this builders had been estimating their own quantities.

Then the government, to avoid being thought of as favouring any one contractor, started selecting their contractors on the sole basis of cost. Private developers often followed suit. Designers were still being selected on the basis of merit (or who they knew) and were being paid agreed percentages of the costs of building, but it became clear that this was also about to change, and did so. There were attempts to avoid selection of the design team purely on the basis of cost, such as a two envelope system the Architectural Division introduced, but this led to dissension from low tenderers so it was abandoned.

The entire construction team of designers, contractors and suppliers became selected on cost.

For construction, a team game that requires all parts to put their best efforts into designing and building for economical excellence, this was, and is, a disaster. No other team game would dream of selecting its side on how much each player was to charge. I was opposed to the selection on price and said so publically. It is a recipe that pushes each party into limiting its inputs to a minimum, avoiding responsibilities as much as possible, and avoiding the costs of comparing design possibilities to achieve optimum results. I thought it would lead to design teams cutting their design time, not reviewing possible alternatives, lowering the quality and coverage of documentation, squabbling, shedding of as much responsibility as possible by all those involved and to expensive legal battles, as it has. There were still design and construction teams selected on merit in the private sector, and occasionally by Design and Construct packages, but the main contracts were, and are, based on cost. It is my opinion that the only beneficiaries of the selection of the design and construction teams by cost are those involved in the inevitable disputes.

When I was given the responsibility of being in charge of a design team, I persuaded clients such as Osborne Metal Industries, Readymix Concrete, Alcoa and Peters Ice Cream to allow me to form a team of designers based on performance, not fees, and occasionally, to select a head contractor based on track record and site personnel to be seconded to the project. Once the team was assembled the basis of the charges for all members was agreed. The team then worked together to arrive at optimum design results. Sub-contract packages were put together and let to preferred sub-contractors and suppliers after they had been selected by the head contractor, the QS and the designers for the package being let, from a short list of quality sub-contractors and suppliers. The successful sub-contractor or supplier was not selected purely on the basis of cost but on the criteria of value for money and value to the contract. The packages were limited so that if a party selected proved unsatisfactory they were not included when the next package was let. All the projects constructed on that basis went well, finished on time and below budget, and all parties enjoyed building them. Quality produced was high and team spirit prevailed. Added bonuses were that the head contractors were involved in design decisions so that economies were made and it was possible to overlap early construction work with the detailed design phase.

It is probable that, because I was fortunate enough for my early career to have been with the Architectural Division of the Public Works Department, with its own day labour force who worked with the architectural and engineering designers, and who were only too happy to criticize design shortcomings, that I learnt that construction was a team game, as it is. Good teams are not created by limiting the cost of the services to be provided or by pitting parts of the team against other parts, as selection on price does.

Those making the decision to select on price did not consider the possible, subtle consequences that could result when they decided that selection on price was the optimum selection approach. They did not consider the cost of the legal battles that would result, the time that would be wasted, the quality of design and construction that would be lost, and that if a builder became bankrupt, what effect that would have on the costs, and the added time, of completing unfinished buildings. Despite the advantages of selection on merit, and the shortcomings of selection on cost, clients, especially government clients, have continued with selection on price.

As these events were taking place it became apparent that disputes would arise, so a settlement forum was needed. Arbitration became an increasing part of the building scene. Initially arbitrators were retired builders and experienced designers – architects and engineers of various disciplines. Arbitration courts sat and listened to both sides of disputes and made binding decisions, not all of which were received with agreement by both parties to the dispute.

Because nearly all parties to disputes carried insurances or indemnities, and because the insurers and indemnifiers did not trust their insured to protect their insurance dollar when they could gain favour with a client by admitting responsibility, two things happened. The first was that those indemnified were not allowed to admit liability, even if they were clearly responsible, and the second was that the insurers were to have their funds protected by independent lawyers. The presentation of the positions of both sides of any dispute were to be provided by lawyers trained to argue points of law, many of whom did not, and do not, understand the subtleties of construction, the mechanics of materials or the complexities of building systems. Another group also arose – technical experts who were providing courts with their understanding of the issues involved. I know this group. I have been one of them. Not all provide their evidence in a disinterested manner. Some act as advocates. It is difficult not to accentuate the positive and attempt to eliminate the negative when your client is paying you. Not all experts understand the complexities with which they are faced, and experts who do understand them sometimes have difficulties in explaining complex technical matters to the arbitrators and judges they are supposed to be informing. Good communicators have the ability to sell a doubtful thesis to non-technical persons. Settlement of construction disputes has become a battlefield of insurers with their expensive knights from the legal fraternity battling it out, aided by amenable experts. That is the situation today.

The system has basic flaws. There is nothing driving the litigants and lawyers conducting a case to come to a rapid conclusion. Insurers do not have to meet remediation costs until a final decision against them is made and the longer a matter takes to be settled the greater the lawyer's fee. This is not to say that many litigants and their lawyers deliberately drag cases out but it has been known to happen.

Several years ago I was involved in a complex case of structural failure. I suggested to the lawyer who had engaged me – an honourable man who became a High Court judge – that I hold discussions with his opposition's expert to see if there were areas on which we could reach agreement. He agreed. The opposition's lawyer would not allow the meeting. The case was heard before a very clever and balanced judge who understood the technical issues, and having heard the evidence found in favour of the case put forward by the lawyer I was advising. The opposition lawyer appealed the finding and, again, lost. Except that he did not lose. He gained. His client lost. When the case was over the opposition's expert approached me and asked if we could discuss the issues. We did and found that we were in agreement on many of the matters in contention, and that an earlier meeting would have helped shorten the court hearing.

## Issues and Challenges

Another case, of which I know, that displays some of the shortcomings of the present system in dealing with fairly simple construction shortcomings, concerns a young couple who wanted to demolish part of an old residence for a new extension. Their estimated costs, for what they wanted done, were less than $25,000. Their neighbour objected because, in his view, what they were having done would have an adverse impact on his property. He provided no specific issues, but referred to a section of the Building Act, which, in part, covers 'structural integrity'. He also employed an architect and a structural engineer who each prepared a report that the young couple's expert considered were based on conjectures, as no verifiable facts were presented. No specific arguments that what was proposed was deleterious to the neighbour's property, and no supporting evidence that it was, were presented. However, because their reports backed the neighbour's claim the matter escalated. The couple's expert considered that had the neighbour's architect and their engineer advised their client that the problems with what was being done were not only minor but questionable, the dispute could have been settled quickly and at minimal cost.

The young couple's plans had been approved by the local authority but there were still problems. The neighbour objected to work going ahead and the matter was heard by a magistrate. The neighbour also refused to allow the couple's expert, to examine his property for basic flaws or shortcomings so that matter was also put before a magistrate's court. Costs were incurred. The referrals to courts resulted in 15 months of unnecessary legal procedures. The neighbour employed a barrister forcing the young couple to also employ a barrister. Both the young couple's barrister and the magistrate appeared to have limited understanding of building matters but the magistrate did order that the young couple's expert could inspect the neighbour's property.

According to the young couple's expert their barrister concentrated on legalities, not on the practicalities of building and its affects. The neighbour's architect brought up many issues that the couple's expert considered to be irrelevant, during the hearing.

As I write this, it is four and a half months since the hearing closed and there is, as yet, no finding. The cost to the young couple for the hearing has been very high, and they have been forced to meet the continuing cost of rental accommodation. Their costs of the disagreements to date will certainly far exceed the costs of the young couple's proposed works. Their expert considers that the matter has been handled in an absurdly expensive manner and should never have been put to a magistrate's court hearing, but to a hearing of a more appropriate court such as the State Administration Tribunal, who have a much better understanding of construction issues.

Who has benefited from what has happened? Not the young couple who, I have been informed, have acted with integrity. Their expenses have been high. The beneficiaries have been lawyers, the courts and the experts. Is this justice?

There are lessons to be learnt from these, and other, cases.

- Not all experts are equal. Some of the best minds capable of understanding abstruse technical issues are not able to express those issues in terms that legal minds can grasp, whereas some experts are able to confidently present what is actually shaky evidence in a manner that makes it believable.
- Judges, steeped as they are in the complexities and subtleties of the law, are probably not the best people to decide on difficult technical issues. This is not to denigrate judges. Architects and engineers are, similarly, not experts on the intricacies of the law.
- Technical issues should be settled by agreement if at all possible. They should not be subjected to the adversarial legal system, and they should not be decided by those trained in the legal processes but by those with experience in design and construction. It is unlikely that this will be agreed to by the legal fraternity.
- The costs and time absorbed by the current approaches to settling construction disputes are very high. Court costs, lawyer's fees and the costs of expert witnesses can be so great that they can, and do, outrun the cost of remedying the shortcoming.

Is there an alternative? In my view we should be attempting to return to a modified form of the old round table conference, and trying to sort out why the problems have arisen, instead of all those involved hiding in their legal bunkers, admitting nothing and having their experts attempting to score points. Given today's adversarial approach to settling what can be complex technical disagreements, and the fact that insurers will not allow clients to admit liability, even if it is obvious where responsibilities lie, there is little chance of a round table approach being acceptable. This means that it is necessary that there be decisions taken by a disinterested tribunal.

Currently the deciding tribunal is an arbitration court, a court of law, or the State Administrative Tribunal with arbitrators, magistrates or judges hearing arguments put forward by lawyers and experts attempting to protect their client's interests. This is an expensive procedure. Perhaps a better, fairer and more economical approach would be for a select group of, say, 15 people with experience in various areas of design and construction, and who are not in positions that would colour their decisions, being selected based on their experiences and track records. Care will have to be taken with the selection of this panel. The group should be formed from contractors and sub-contractors no longer engaged in commercial dealings, quantity surveyors who are still active but not engaged in commercial undertakings and semi-retired architects and engineers with experience in various disciplines. Those chosen must have records of quality buildings and impeccable honesty with their handling of contracts and disputes. It is not necessary that they are publically prominent or important but it is necessary that they have experience and integrity. I have not included lawyers on the grounds that if the matter is purely a legal one, not a technical one, it should be handled by the current adversarial system.

When a technical dispute arises that cannot be settled by discussion, it can be put before the panel, who would then select three of their number who were most experienced in the area of the dispute, to hear the arguments. The cases could then be put to the three by those involved in the dispute, and their technical advisors – not by lawyers. Other experts or lawyers could be called by the three tribunal members, if they consider they would be helpful. Having heard the evidence the trio would make decisions that are binding.

The outcomes and costs of settling disputes by an expert tribunal in this manner would, almost certainly, be fairer than the present system, and will certainly be a great deal less expensive.

There is little doubt that this suggested approach will be resisted by those who currently gain financial benefits from the existing systems. Also, there is always inertia in the construction industry. It will be interesting to hear why this suggested system is inferior to the existing ponderous systems, and what its flaws are considered to be.

# SECTION 5

# MISCELLANEOUS MATTERS

I am a structural engineer, so my main interests lie in logical solutions to structural problems. Therefore the discussions in this section mostly deal with what I regard as problem areas. I have introduced a part of my young, personal history to give any reader who might be interested some of the background that has led me to where I am. I feel privileged to have lived in Australia in the period after the Second World War, when Australia was developing and optimistically energetic. I now worry that we in Australia have lost our toughness, our energy, our ability to make do, and our earlier pioneering spirit; our independence. To me it appears we consider we are due for higher rewards for less effort. I am concerned that the expectations of our society are now greater than it is prepared, and able, to produce. Or is my pessimism just a product of my old age?

## 42. THE MEDIA'S ROLES AND RESPONSIBILITIES.

The media has several functions, the most important of which is the responsibility of investigating the activities of humanity, both locally and globally, and reporting on these activities in a balanced manner. Unbalanced reporting is propaganda. To meet its responsibilities the media has to investigate the background of human activities with the object of bringing to light the motives behind the actions that have been taken. Having thoroughly investigated and having arrived at positions based on the evidence, the media then has the responsibility of presenting its findings in a disinterested manner – that is in a manner without bias. Is this how the reporting media of the world carries out its duties?

Obviously the individuals carrying out the reporting are entitled to their personal beliefs and views on religious, political, racial, legal and moral matters, but they should put these aside when reporting to the public. The reporting media have a leading role, perhaps the leading role, in shaping public opinion. This gives it the responsibility of providing background facts and conclusions from those facts that are as balanced as possible. Those reporting are not entitled to report only those facts that agree with their personal positions or ignoring, or hiding, facts that favour a different interpretation. They have a duty to be impartial.

The reporting media also has the testing responsibility of following up matters of public interest that are hidden, sometimes by those in positions of authority. The investigations of bank charges, and insurance and investment fees are cases where the questions that have been asked should have been asked long ago. There are other areas of concern that need investigation. As an instance I wonder what would be uncovered if a fully empowered and unbiased investigation was made into who benefits financially, and to what degree they benefit, from public and union superannuation funds. There is no doubt that the reporting media has a great deal of responsibility and has high standards to meet. Is it meeting those standards as it should?

Having said that the reporting media has the duty of impartiality I now make it clear that it is quite reasonable to publish opinion pieces by those who take positions on religious, political, racial, legal or moral matters, as long as they make it clear where they stand and that they are not attempting to be impartial. So the publishing and broadcasting media has the twofold role of investigating and reporting, in an impartial manner, on the activities of humanity, and of providing platforms for those with points of view to air their positions and to give their reasons for adopting the positions they have taken.

The media have, of course, other roles to fulfil. All media outlets, with the exception of those financed by governments, have to be able to support themselves financially. They do this by printing or broadcasting items that they think will attract the public and by selling advertising space. For financial success they need audiences, so they generally concentrate on shallow entertainments – the doings of stars, food preparation, sporting competitions, entertainment competitions, quizzes, house building and renovation, family shows, crime and crime solving and, of course, the immediate news of today as sifted through some editor's view of the world. Occasionally there are educational entertainments, such as those of Brian Cox or David Attenborough, on television, and adult and children's puzzles and quizzes in magazines and newspapers, and there are forums where opinions are expressed and discussed. The media probably consider they are following the demands of the public but it is likely that rather than following public tastes the media are leading the public taste as much in democracies as propaganda machines are leading populations in less liberal societies. Remember Goebbels and consider Xi.

As you can see I have some sympathy for privately owned and operated media outlets showing biases and attracting audiences with entertainments of doubtful value, but for those outlets funded by the taxpayers of Australia – the SBS and the ABC – there is no excuse. They are obliged to show all sides of any controversial issue, especially matters that cannot be readily checked factually, but are faith and belief based. If the ABC or the SBS is to feature a Christian providing points of view it should also feature a Moslem, a follower of the Jewish religion and, even, an atheist providing their points of view and the reasons behind them. If moral issues such as same sex relationships, abortion, euthanasia, killing in conflicts and appropriate punishments for crimes are to be aired they must also cover dissenting views, and the reasons for those views should be discussed. If political, legal or racial arguments are put forward they must, similarly, have conflicting points of view aired, and the discussions should be based on the situations of today – not the situations of 2000, or even 200, years ago. Humanity has to look forward to the future and how it can best exist in productive peace. It can look back at the past in an attempt to avoid repeating mistakes but it cannot change history and it should not allow past injustices to racial groups such as the Red Indians, or to religious groups such as the Jews, to give those groups special treatment. All should be treated equally.

Humans, being the emotionally driven creatures that they so often are – creatures that have been subjected to conflicting religious and moral teachings when their psyche was being formed – can find it difficult to accept tenets that differ from those they have absorbed. Then there are the variabilities of human minds. Not all humans have the same reasoning power, and not all are logical and balanced. Some are psychologically disturbed and some are brain damaged. So complete balance is unlikely to be achieved by the media. Though this is so the media, especially the publically funded media, must strive for balance and those controlling the outputs of the publically funded media must not allow their personal beliefs and learnings to interfere with presenting as balanced a presentation as possible.

# 43. AUSTRALIA – PAST, PRESENT and FUTURE.

Australia is, almost certainly, one of the better places in the world in which to live at this time. Is it getting better as a place to live or is it deteriorating? Currently it has a population who, in the main, are reasonably healthy and long lived – although obesity is now common – adequate food, clean water, reticulated electrical power (although this is not as reliable as it should be), sound buildings, reasonable infrastructures, and a society that has access to transport, sufficient wealth to reward those who are interested in providing for society's needs, and that even provides funds for those who do not wish to work or cannot. It also provides opportunities for those who make the effort to take those opportunities, a reasonable education system for those who wish to learn, and a reasonably fair, if ponderous and expensive, legal system. This quality of life did not come about without effort by many in the past. We should now consider whether or not we can reasonably expect our generous lifestyle to continue, given the present performances of parts of our society.

How did Australia arrive at the privileged position it now holds? Would it have become the nation it has if it had not been invaded by Europeans? Would others, perhaps less humane than the Europeans who did invade, have taken over from that group who have lived on the island continent for at least 50,000 years without building permanent settlements, have produced a fairer society? The history of the world is awash with conquerors who have behaved badly and wiped out tribes they have defeated. Has the English invasion been completely detrimental to those Australians related to the original inhabitants, or have those related to the original indigenes who, I understand, now outnumber the population when Cook landed, gained advantages from the invaders? As there were crimes against the aborigines committed by some of the early invaders, and as they have been treated shamefully at times in the past, is it reasonable, or even possible, to attempt to redress these old mistreatments by treating those with aboriginal blood differently to the progeny of the invaders who have completely changed Australia into its modern form? Should we not, as a society with a mixed heritage, concentrate on each of us contributing to our mixed society as best as each of us can and not dwell on past wrongs? There are many questions and as many points of view. I am not an historian and I am not in a position to answer these questions, but my 87 year history might provide a snap shot of interest, and it might point to where we are currently heading.

My grandfather Walter was a German mining engineer who, with his Swiss wife and a baby son (my father) migrated to Zeehan in Tasmania to work at its silver-lead mine near the turn of the 20th century. They were brave and hardy people. The growing family left Zeehan to be part of the exploitation of the riches of Paddy Hannan's gold find at Kalgoorlie in 1893. Walter was hurt in a mining accident, became consumptive and was hospitalised at Woorooloo, but not before his family had grown to eight children – 5 girls and 3 boys. Although young, my father became head of the family that moved to Ewing Street Welshpool, then well out on the fringe of Perth, into a timber framed 'weatherboard' four roomed house with semi-enclosed verandahs on three sides on which all slept, during hot summers and cold winters. Although scheme water was reticulated to the site for watering the garden, a tank gathering water from the galvanised iron roof supplied water to the kitchen and the bathroom. The kitchen had a small table with chairs and a basin in one corner next to a Metters No. 2 oven for which I, later, had to light the fire, and provide the chopped wood. The flooring was linoleum on timber boarding some metre above the sloping ground. In my time there an ice-chest looked after perishables in summer. The bathroom was an enclosed section of the back verandah. It had a painted (eau de nil) galvanised iron bath that drained into the garden, and a chip burning bath heater, also painted. Saturday night was bath night. Down the back stairs was the washhouse, with its twin concrete troughs separated by a diaphragm, on which was perched an ancient, hand operated wringer. The washhouse was slightly protected by a wall of honeysuckle vine on a wire mesh screen. Washing was done in an adjacent copper fired by chopped wood. After being brought to the boil the washing was rinsed in the troughs, then wrung out and hung on two clothes lines supported at each end by a timber arm that swivelled on a bolt that passed through a 6 inch by 6 inch post, and at mid-point by timber props bought from an itinerant Aborigine. The copper was emptied by bucket, in my time by me, and the soapy water poured onto the garden.

Behind a clump of bamboos, some distance from the back stairs, was an outdoor toilet that had its pan changed weekly. It was into this house that my sister, my father and I moved to live with my grandmother after the break-up of the marriage of my parents. If, today, anyone was offered that house in pristine condition they would look at the person who offered it as though they were insane – but those were the living conditions just a lifetime ago, and our house was not the house that had the poorest facilities in the street, it was among the best.

The early schooling of my, younger, sister and me, along with the Gales, the Pantings, the Robinsons and other, young Welshpool residents such as Alf Lyons, Fred Wren and Jimmy Hurley, was in a timber hall building next to Welshpool Road, where Miss Brady did her best to equip years 1, 2 and 3 with the rudiments of English, history, geography, mathematics and even literature, poetry and music. The hall was also used one night a week for playing table tennis, quoits and darts by the young locals, and later by Mick Tilby for showing that wonder – movies – and serving steaming hot dogs from a large pot at interval. Mick and George Milne went on to develop 'The Bright Spot' and sell hamburgers and other delights from caravans at the junction of Canning Highway and Mill Point Road and at the Claremont Speedway.

## Issues and Challenges

After Grade 3 we had to walk the mile to Queens Park State School in bare feet both in summer, when tar melted on the narrow strip of Welshpool Road, and in winter, when there was still frost on the grass beside the road. The Welshpool troupe of the Gales, the Robinsons and the Pantings, all of whom lived in Ewing Street, ensured there was always company for the walk. Some days our walk coincided with the local milkman, Stan Smith, driving his horse drawn cart home at the end of his round. We would all jog behind his cart and occasionally he would offer one of us a lift on the board at the rear of his cart. The lucky passenger would smirk down on the rapidly tiring joggers. At school we were joined by the market gardening, Greek contingent of the Psaltis's, the Lucas's, the Pauls, Manuel Manolas, Manuel Cjuglas, Frankie Buttergig and sundry other children – the Humbles, Bruce Doyle, the MacMillans, Bill Mc Neill, Ray Beard, the Comelys, George Edwards, the Smallhorns, Mary Davies, Florrie Harwood, and the Scottish contingent, Don McDonald and his sister Margaret. Then there was the special group who lived next door at Sister Kate's home. Thanks to Sir Ronald Wilson they are now known as the Stolen Generation. Some believe they were the rescued generation. We all had one thing in common – we were all Australians and proud of it. Of the Sister Kate contingent only the blonde-headed Gerry Warber was in my class but coming after us there were people who became football stars – Ted Kilmurray and Graham "Polly" Farmer. We were a mixed bag and there were occasional frictions, but we generally got along even though we played some rough games.

Teaching facilities were basic. Classrooms were neither heated in winter nor cooled in summer. All our English headmaster, Mr. Bumstead, had to help him and his staff in teaching their motley classes were blackboards, chalk and dusters. The teachers tried hard, and we learnt in spite of ourselves. The teachers were aided by the fact that in those days we children did not know we had the right to express our personalities as children now do, so we were quiet as "Dagwood", Miss Thayer and Miss Matthews went about their teaching duties and we remained fairly disciplined. I do not recall even one class disruption. Things have changed (for the better?). At that time if a child went home and told its parents it had been caned at school, a rare event, they would more than likely not have received a sympathetic hearing. No parent would have dreamed of starting a war with the headmaster.

In lunch hours we boys played Red Rover All Over, wrestled each other off a fallen log, or had cockfights between larger boys carrying smaller boys. My horse was the gallant Con' Psaltis as we tried to pull each other down. Sometimes we played Brandy with a tennis ball that we threw at each other. It was the only game we played where being small, as I was, helped. As can be seen our games were not politically correct, but political correctness had not then been invented. No one got really hurt. The girls were much more refined, as girls were in those times. They played Hop Scotch. Sport for boys was cricket on a concrete pitch in summer and soccer on a sand area in winter. Both games were played in bare feet. There was a war going on so we boys dug slit trenches in the grey sand for our protection in the event of an air raid. They were never used. Could it be said that it was all good character building stuff?

After Grade 6 we all trooped off to High School. Many of the Queens Park boys went to Kent Street High School. I finished up at Forrest High School, then in Lord Street, East Perth. To get there involved taking the steam engined train from Welshpool to East Perth and then walking the mile to the school, this time in shoes. There were other boys from further up the Armadale line on the train, and even a couple from Carlisle and Victoria Park. We were joined by boys from the Midland line and some locals. Early on we were separated into classes – 7A to 7D to 9A to 9D. The teacher of 7A was Charlie Lenanton, a returned serviceman, who had quiet command. We learnt from him and we also suffered the pangs of puberty at different times as we each matured. We played Brandy and skittles in our lunch hours, and football, cricket and baseball on an adjacent park on sports days. We were a mixed crew. Len Cannell went on to be a prominent jockey. Des Gibson became an executive of Gibbs Bright. Doug' Costello became the principal of a Technical College. One 7D student in our year was a loner who would not join us in our games. His name was Eric Cook. He was the last person to be hanged in Western Australia, for multiple murders.

I formed a particular friendship with Jim Stephen of Gosnells that lasted for several years. Jim's father had been killed in the Second World War. We all duly sat for our Junior Certificate and went on to different schools to do our Leaving Certificate.

Jim and I went to Leederville Technical School, which had just opened and which involved catching a train to Perth and a tram out to Oxford Street. In summer I sometimes rode my bicycle from Welshpool to "Leedy", helped by a following easterly wind and then home aided by the Fremantle Doctor. Passing through Victoria Park I sometimes picked up Lindsay Dadd, a farmer's son living with a policeman's family, and we rode together. At Leederville Tech' there was a mixed bag of boys, girls and some returned servicemen, both Australian ex-servicemen (Syd' Bowater and Dusty Miller) and Americans (Dean Spencer, Ray Jones and Darryl Burt, who had married Australian girls). Jim and I were young and not very academic, so lectures played a secondary role to playing snooker down at the billiard hall attached to the hotel on the corner of Newcastle Street, and listening to the stories Jack Lekias told us at his fish and chip shop in Lord Street.

Despite the distractions, I decided to attend guest lectures on Practical Plain and Solid Geometry given by Erich Wolfgang Shilbury. It proved to be a turning point for my future career. He was a Jewish structural engineer who had escaped from Germany with his family when he saw that Hitler was going to pursue his hatred of the Jews. He was a man who expected much from himself and from his students. For some reason he took a liking to me. Years later, after I had graduated from Mr. Shilbury's engineering school at Perth Technical College as a structural engineer and when I was lecturing to night school classes for him, I asked him why he bothered with the flighty and juvenile student I had been and he told me "I saw potential". He had better eye sight than most of my other lecturers. He was a clever and dedicated man and I am everlastingly grateful to him.

Encouraged by my father, Jim and I rode our bicycles, loaded down with a tent, sleeping bags, water bottles and a variety of tinned food around the south west of the state in August 1949 when I turned 17. It was a great adventure and I still remember it well. I wonder if a parent would encourage a son to do such a trip today. That Christmas of 1949 I worked at Boans, then the biggest department store in Perth, bagging nuts and making up Christmas orders for customers, in the Grocery and Provisions Department, for the princely sum of 25 shillings a week.

During the Christmas breaks, we students nearly all looked for temporary work. In 1950, together with other students and a couple of young men who had recently been released from gaol after serving a sentence for sacking the offices of the Communist Party, I went to Corrigin to work for Cooperative Bulk Handling under the guidance of a construction foreman named Neil Pickersgill, a quintessential Aussie. Early in the cropping season, we laid floors in bins and bulkheads, which were wheat storages, by laying sand and binding it with tar-like materials called Colas and Terolas that were sprayed. Because we were spraying these materials and because conditions were usually windy, we all got caught by the spray drift, so we were known, for good reason, as "The Black Gang". We bounced from wheat collection centre to wheat collection centre – that is from bin to bin – over rudimentary and badly corrugated roads in the back of a flatbed truck, and we slept on the ground or in the wheat in our sleeping bags after having washed the black goo off with dieseline. Later, in the hot summer season, after much of the wheat had been delivered, we put roofs onto the heaped wheat in the bulkheads by driving stakes into the sloping mounds, as we waded knee deep and shirtless in the wheat in the scorching sun. Onto the stakes, which had holes bored through them near their tops, we placed timbers. Onto the timbers we put sheets of hot corrugated galvanised iron, and on them timber battens to secure them. The whole was then held together with wire twitches. I suppose it was tough, but we enjoyed working in our bare feet and shorts and we thought that the pay was wonderful. Now that the world has advanced we would need to wear protective clothing, face masks to prevent us inhaling wheat dust, and steel capped boots, and we would have to be strapped into seat belts to travel. Our world has improved.

One particularly oppressive afternoon, just after the team had climbed down from the top of the wheat-filled Corrigin bulkhead for tea, a vicious willie-willie – a mini-tornado – came suddenly through and lifted our newly placed section of roof and carried it away like a giant kite, with its stakes dangling from it like insect's legs, to crash down a hundred metres away. Had we been still on it we would have learned how to fly.

Following my introduction to the collection of the precious grain on the Black Gang, the following Christmas of 1951, when I was 19, I was given my own weighbridge at Nornakin, 9 miles out of Corrigin, where I weighed trucks as they came in and as they exited, having discharged their golden cargo, and tallied their total deliveries. I was known as the weighbridge officer. A fresh-faced, recent arrival from England named Arthur Stevenson was the bin attendant. To get to Nornakin, I rode my recently purchased, £50, 1936 500cc V twin BSA motor cycle, with its unsprung rear and its girder forks, over some of the most diabolical corrugated roads the world has ever experienced. My back still twinges. In the weeks that followed, I fell off the V twin several times on loose gravel without doing much damage, and Arthur once jumped off the pillion when he thought I was going to crash when we got into a wild slide (I did not). He was not going to have his hide burnt by red hot exhaust pipes. He badly damaged his elbow. Then he had to get back onto the pillion to be taken into Corrigin to Doctor Jones, who was no friend of motorcycles even though they provided him with patients.

We cooked over an open fire, showered under a shower bucket suspended from a timber beam between the wheat bin and our water tank that contained rain water from the bin roof well-seasoned with parrot droppings and wheat dust, and slept on camp stretchers in the open. Because of the heat we could not keep anything for more than a day. Occasionally we managed to shoot a rabbit that we then cleaned, cooked and ate. The farmers, our customers, were wonderful and occasionally brought us titbits and cold beers, and we helped them unload their bags of wheat. Screw conveyors were just coming into general use, so most loads came in bags that had to be dragged across the flat beds of the trucks and carefully tipped into the hopper attached to the bottom of our elevator, which then delivered the wheat into the top of our bin. Both Arthur and I thought that the hardships were more than made up for by the wages and the friendliness of our 'cockies'.

By the standards of today, it was awfully rough and ready – but was it really? By today's standards we were subjected to unsafe working conditions and primitive living conditions with our open fire and no toilet facilities, but how damaging was it? Perhaps it helped toughen our generation up. My father certainly thought that the conditions under which I lived were comfortable when compared to his early days, given my camp stretcher and my sleeping bag.

When Nornakin ran out of deliveries, Lance Ainsworth, the district supervisor for Cooperative Bulk Handling, posted me to Yealering to tidy up there – but that is another story, a story of romance with a farmer's daughter, of learning to drink with some fine people and of me being put in my place. I loved it all.

My final year of weighing wheat was at Trayning in 1952, the year I graduated. There, I lived with the butcher and his wife, drank far too much with the local larrikins, and learnt how to lose money by betting on trotters at the Merredin Raceway. There were some unique characters such as Porky and Jumbo Cooper, and two, not one but two, bin attendants; Eric Allpike and Don Harper. I look fondly back on those experiences and on the people I was lucky enough to have been associated with. Australians then expected less and were prepared to contribute more – or is that just my rose-coloured imagination?

It was a time of my life when I was optimistic about the future. The war was over and rationing had faded. Our side had won and we were going to build a better world. My fellow students and I believed that we could make a difference. I had spent a good deal of my time during my engineering training with architectural students because they were my age, and many of my fellow engineering students were older and were returned servicemen. I thought highly of several of the young, putative architects. That high opinion has been found to be accurate, as several have gone on to contribute some fine works to the built environment, and I have had the privilege of being involved as the structural consultant for a good proportion of their creations, such as several university buildings, several high schools, the office buildings Central Park and Exchange Plaza, the grandstands at the WACA ground and the original Forrest Place re-development.

So that was the Australia I grew up in – a country at war for several years, so that there was rationing of butter, sugar, tea and petrol, slit trenches in the school yard and a buried air raid shelter near the fig tree in our back yard, in case of an air attack. A country of few luxuries. The fortunate had little electric radiators over which the family could huddle in winter as they listened to that other luxury, the radio, as it churned out *"Martin's Corner"*, *"Love and Marriage"*, *"Dad and Dave"* and *"First Light Fraser"*. Looking back, and possibly with memories misted by time, I remember it as a country of many interesting individuals, a country where behaving honourably was quietly well thought of and behaving dishonourably was frowned on, where putting effort into the job you were employed to do and earning your keep was widely considered the way to conduct yourself, and where luxuries were few but those we did have, such as Hopalong Cassidy on Saturday nights at the movies, were appreciated.

An early memory is of Woolworths in Hay Street (a Hay Street replete with trams running down its centre) installing a narrow escalator and that other modern wonder, air conditioning. People visited the store just for the joy of being transported effortlessly to another level and breathing in the bliss of cool air on summer days.

Australia was still recovering from a depression when I was young and I gained the distinct impression from family members that those who had accepted support from the government – the dole – were not highly thought of. All of my father's siblings had managed to find work. There was obviously a vastly different morality then to the morality of today, when many expect, and get, financial help from the government. There was then a degree of righteousness in the community but there was also a willingness in the community to help in a quiet and unobtrusive manner. (My grandmother knitted many pairs of socks for soldiers away at the war and my father, as he had the only car in Ewing Street, provided transport when it was needed). My father worked long hours on such things as the electrical and communications wirings for the wooden submarine chasers known as Fairmiles, being built near the old Causeway as his part of the war effort. The community was then peopled by independent persons who accepted their lot and worked to improve it themselves. I did not once hear anyone say that the government had to fix anything. Expectation levels were not high and the Welshpool community was optimistic

Is Australia now a better place? Is it fairer and more moral in its behaviour and its dealings? Are the citizens as hard working, as honourable, and as resilient? Or has Australia become a society that expects much, that votes itself benefits out of the government's taxation coffers, and that does not perform well enough to merit its standard of living? Because Australians now expect much, and as many perform poorly and believe they are entitled to a share of the wealth they see around them without contributing to its production, are the current standards of living sustainable? Or will Australia's governments continue to spend more than they take to get elected, until they have sold their assets of value and have exhausted the patience of their lenders? Are we approaching another depression?

## 44. ONE AUSTRALIA.

There are now, in Australia, many expecting benefits from the government, and our politicians, our leaders, are obliged to compete for the votes of the over 50% of the population who receive such benefits by making promises that our economy is having difficulty sustaining. This is a recipe for disaster in the longer term. Sooner or later our economy is likely to collapse as it did in the Great Depression. We need less demands from parts of our population and more production by our total population. We need less pandering to minority groups to get their vote, and more effort from those groups. We need a vital and performing One Australia, not a mendicant Australia that expects the government to fix everything and does not take on the challenge of outperforming the rest of the world.

Minority groups must realise that they must help themselves, and that their lives can be worthwhile both for themselves and for their society if they contribute to that mixed society. They should not continue to lead lives believing they are entitled to, relying on, and wasting handouts, as many currently do. . I find it sad that so many people who have untapped capabilities are ruining their lives affected by alcohol and other drugs, paid for by the taxpayers of our country, and are condemning their children to similar wasted lives. Surely a life of effort and production – of raising crops, husbanding animals, building infrastructure, producing art, making artefacts, tending the aged, educating and nurturing the young, and contributing to our society in other ways – would be more fulfilling than spending life in a drug-affected state and subsisting. I do not know how some fell into the mess they are in, and I also do not know how we change the ethos that is destroying so many. It must come from within. The government cannot fix it.

The society of Australia should make it clear that if anyone is lucky enough to be born in Australia, or has come here to live, they all have the same rights and responsibilities. There should be no special privileges granted to a section of the community because of its ethnic origin, its sexual orientation or its religious beliefs. No one is special enough to warrant greater entitlements. No one should expect to receive special benefits from the efforts of others, except those with infirmities.

There are the two sides to the coin of living in a society – rights (and privileges) and responsibilities. For a healthy Australia, and for the benefit of those who come after us, we must be a vibrant and productive society, not one that expects much and contributes poorly – not one that leaves a massive debt.

Each of us has a responsibility to contribute to our society as well as we can, and the right to expect reasonable rewards for our inputs – rewards that reflect the financial state of the country and how it fits in with the rest of the world. No one has the right to rewards from the public purse because of an accident of birth that puts them into a special category, and no one, or no one group, no matter how important, has the right to set themselves ridiculously high salary or reward conditions. However those with physical or psychological frailties should be able to expect the privilege of support from their society, but they must recognise that with this privilege goes the responsibility to contribute as best they can both for the health of their society and for their own well-being and self-esteem. There can be no excuse for those capable of doing so not to contribute. There is no excuse for those sponging on the Australian community when they do not need to and, especially, of sponging on the public purse, or stealing, to support drug and alcohol habits.

## Issues and Challenges

There is a theory that we are all born equal, but this is obviously not so. Some are better equipped physically, some mentally or psychologically, some with physical attractiveness, and some with personalities that are pleasing to others when they are born or as they develop. And some are born with, or develop, damage, both physical and mental. Those fortunate enough to possess superior mental or physical capabilities should make use of their assets for the benefit of both their society and themselves, and those who are damaged can reasonably expect the privilege of support.

In the distant past, in the recent past, and at the present time, there have been and are many examples of societies that have not abided by these reasonable rules. In some societies, groups of the privileged have lived, and now live, lives of ridiculous opulence while the people around them have starved and suffered. An example from the past is the conditions that led to the French Revolution, and examples from today are the several Mugabe mansions and the many extremely expensive cars and jewellery owned by that family.

There have been, and still are, cases where humans were treated differently, and badly, because of the colour of their skins or their religious leanings, and there have been societies where attempts have been made to wipe out groups considered inferior because of their race or their religion. If Australia is to thrive there must not be any specially privileged group or any specially denigrated group. Any such lack of balance must be put behind us. The rights of all must be equal regardless of race, colour, sexual orientation or religious belief. And with those rights must go the responsibility for each individual to contribute to our Australian society to the best of that individual's capacity.

Australia has the opportunity to be an example to the rest of the world for fairness, individual effort and community spirit. It must not allow itself to become a society where unfair practices become ingrained, or where different groups are treated differently. Today we hear much about the rights of various individuals, but we never hear about the responsibilities of those individuals. Why not? Why is our society concentrating on its rights and not on its responsibilities? Why is how the cake is divided more important to our society than how it is produced?

The abandonment of discrimination should apply not only to negative issues, such as regarding some groups as inferior, it must also apply to removing special privileges from groups purely because of their ancestry or some other random cause. I see no reason why any ethnic group, especially ethnic groups who have mingled with others and produced citizens of mixed race, should have special privileges given to them by the society of which they are a part. I was against apartheid in South Africa and I am against racial discrimination in Australia, so I am against special privileges being granted to those who claim aboriginal ancestry, because it is discriminatory. Pouring money from the public purse into aboriginal settlements has proven to be counterproductive and it might be better if it is abandoned, both for the health and well-being of those now being encouraged to be mendicants and for society generally. Australia should treat all its citizens equally. The sins of the past should be buried. They cannot be atoned for by the actions of the present, and guilty consciences for past atrocities cannot be cleared by treating later generations differently to their contemporaries. All Australians should be treated the same. Anything else is discrimination – it is apartheid.

There are, of course, people who, because of a lack of ability, cannot live up to the performance levels of others. These people deserve support, and any worthwhile society is duty bound to provide that support. However, a caring society must be careful it does not encourage people to become mendicants – people who exist by obtaining hand-outs from the rest of society. Everyone should be encouraged to use the talents they have. This is not only so that society benefits but, because they are living a life of service to their community, such people feel more confident – more worthwhile. A balance between helping and smothering must be achieved.

A healthy Australia is one in which all feel equal, are treated equally, and in which its citizens all try to contribute. An Australia in which over one third of its budget is spent on 'welfare' to buy votes is not a healthy nation.

## 45. COMPENSATION.

Currently we live in a society in which many of those who are exposed to dangerous working conditions, from working at heights or with dangerous machinery, who are willing to face the hazards of sporting arenas, especially arenas on which contact sports are conducted, who will be subjected to contact with disease, or who are required to operate in environments that lack safety, and who consider themselves to be damaged by these exposures, either physically or psychologically, claim what has become known as compensation. There are those who have deliberately exposed themselves to damage by absorbing or inhaling drugs of one sort or another, especially cigarette smokers, who also consider they are also entitled to be 'compensated'. Then there are those who are sent into combat by their society, and those who are subjected to frightening and, sometimes, quite revolting experiences when they are young. There are differences in how each of these groups should be treated in my opinion – how each should be 'compensated'. Some have knowingly faced the risks and some have had the risks forced upon them.

Those who have taken a personal decision to expose themselves to dangers and hazards or have been paid to face the dangers, surely must carry the responsibility if they suffer damage, as they have willingly done what they did. Those damaged had the responsibility to insure themselves against damage. It should not be a responsibility of society to provide money, to provide 'compensation'.

Similarly, it is not the responsibility of society to compensate for damage suffered because of voluntary misuse of drugs that cause damage, or for damage suffered from taking part in violent sports. The cost of drug damage should be borne by the suppliers of the drugs and/or by the damaged party, and damage from sporting endeavours should be carried by the sport in which the damage occurred. These sports are, after all, money making ventures. As they are not under the control of society, it is not society's responsibility to pay for any damage they cause.

Those damaged during their involvement in combat for their society are, certainly, a responsibility of their society, and their needs must be borne by their society. They must be provided with sufficient funds to live a life as reasonable as it can be, and they must receive psychological support if it is necessary.

Finally we must consider what should be done in the matter of those abused when they were, or are, young. If, as is likely, mistreated young have lasting damage, society must help those who have been damaged.

The Concise Oxford English Dictionary says that compensation is something awarded to compensate for loss, suffering or injury. In our society, compensation is rarely sympathy, moral support or physical repair – it is almost always money. I do not believe that money is the right compensation for the victims of physical damage or sexual predation, although it is often money that victims seek. Giving money to those who have been subjected to molestation by sexual predators seems heartless to me, and for victims to ask for and receive money for their ugly experiences appears to be selling those experiences for cash. Similarly I find it quite repulsive for relatives to claim money as compensation for the loss of a family member. Cash is no substitute for the loss of a loved one or for help to return to a normal life.

When physically and psychologically damaged people are awarded money for their past trials – physical damage, pain and suffering, being denied normal contact with society, being forced into servitude, suffering damage due to unsafe working conditions and, especially, being subjected to the attentions of a sexual predator – is money the right compensation? I do not consider that it is, but when compensation is reported it is almost always reported as money. I find it of interest that victims always want money – not kindness and care, not nourishing food and comfortable surroundings, not warmth and congenial company – only money. Perhaps they consider that money can buy them these things. I do not believe it can. My own view is that money is cold compensation for suffering, so I am at a loss as to why it is so popular. Money is not the right recompense for a foreshortened or damaged life, for suffering, or for a ghastly experience. Surely there are better compensations.

There are circumstances in which money is of little benefit to the sufferer and in which the awarding of a large sum to a damaged person has little value. Such a circumstance is that of a person suffering from a terminal disease such as mesothelioma. Whilst it is not possible to put a monetary value on a foreshortened life, what a person should leave to that person's beneficiaries is not wealth gained from a compensation package. There is something morally wrong, in my opinion, in relatives benefitting monetarily from the suffering of a mortally wounded person. Currently, money claims for the loss of a relative appear to be confined to cases where that relative has expired while being held in detention, but if such claims are successful it is likely that they will spread to money claims for deaths that have been due to vehicle and other accidents. This might be a boon to the legal profession, but it will not help unite our society.

There have been cases of very large awards of money being made to sufferers of health issues that they have brought upon themselves. The prime example is lung cancer brought on by the smoking of cigarettes. No doubt the awards have not been made as compensation for the suffering of the person but as punishment to the shareholders of, and those who operated the company that was sued, but have they been reasonable? When I was a boy, over 75 years ago, my father smoked cigarettes and called them "coffin nails". People knew cigarettes were harmful but they continued with their nicotine habit anyway. The question is – should such reckless behaviour be rewarded with large sums of money, especially money that is going to be spent by relatives of the beneficiaries once they have passed away? I see value in making those who profited from selling the cigarettes suffer financially, but have the right people been punished and was the money channelled into the right direction? And why, as it is clear that smoking is, as the advertisements say, a health hazard, have the various governments not made the selling of cigarettes illegal? Are governments more concerned with allowing people to destroy themselves than they are with preserving them, or is it possibly the money smokers pour into government coffers? Making smoking illegal will not stop addicts smoking, prohibition has never worked, but it would possibly cut the habit to a trickle. My own view is that smokers should be allowed to smoke and the cost of smoking should be high, as it is, to pay for the treatments the smokers will need as the habit overtakes them.

The matter of compensation, especially monetary compensation, is an emotional issue and my views will not be universally agreed. Part of the driving force for money as compensation is reward for the damaged party, and part is punishment for the vendors of destructive substances or actions, with beneficiaries of the beneficiaries being in favour of the present money hand-outs. The system of awarding money to sufferers is of doubtful benefit to them. The matter needs to be discussed in an unemotional manner, and decisions made as to the best means of preventing diseases that foreshorten life, but that can be eliminated with reasonable behaviour, what compensation should be for some of the trials through which people are put, and how the earth can be made a safer and better place to live without destroying the challenges of life that we all need to face in order to grow.

## 46. REASONING VERSUS EMOTION.

A major problem that besets atheists is that if there is no day of judgement – no supreme court that decides whether or not an individual has behaved well enough to be given the benefit of everlasting life in paradise – why should individuals behave well? Why should they not give in to their worst impulses? Why should they not steal, pillage, treat others as chattels, and take what they want by force from those who are weaker? Unless you are attempting to gain an everlasting life in paradise and avoid purgatory, why should you live in a reasonable and civilised manner? Religions are based on life of the 'soul' continuing after death.

The reason why we should behave reasonably is, of course, that only if by far the bulk of humanity lives in a manner that does not damage others many, including the individuals who are committing the crimes, will be damaged. Civilisation requires people to contribute to their society and to behave reasonably – not to steal from or damage others. Those who do not behave in a manner that avoids damaging others, and there are many of those, are attacking the roots of the civilisation under which they live. For civilisation to survive requires that we live in an orderly manner. Living peaceably and contributing to your society is not so that you get to heaven, it is because it is the only way to live that is reasonable, and that will provide enjoyable living conditions for most. It is my belief that if the young Moslem terrorists of this world did not believe they were sealing their place in paradise by obeying their Qur'an and making war on the infidels, and instead understood that they were courting a painful death with no follow up, they would not be so enthusiastic about complying with their brain washing, middle aged imams.

There is still a part of human nature that is a left over from a past when survival and the continuation of the tribe required dominance – greater intelligence, speed, strength and more sophisticated weapons – that is not a good fit with our present close-knit and crowded civilisations. The stupidity of developing ever more sophisticated weapons continues. Seeing the misguided Kim of North Korea showing his absolute delight at the power of his rockets and listening to Trump with his militant statements, I worry about our globe's future. Fortunately, not all countries or humans are threateningly warlike, and many of our finer developments are not destructive.

An example of a non-destructive manifestation of the urge to compete is being a player in, or a supporter of, a sporting team or being a competing individual. Who has not enjoyed a win by their team or felt a frisson of pleasure when their country's athlete wins an Olympic event? Destructive competition comes to the fore when business is conducted in a predatory manner and someone takes more from their society than they have earned. This is often applauded as smart business – but is it? Is it not, really, nasty greed? Why is it admirable to take more than a reasonable reward? Is cheating beneficial to anyone involved? When the competitive nature of we humans is destructive, it damages both those perpetrating the offences, and those damaged by the offences, financially, morally, psychologically and/or physically.

Instead of measured discussion based on the facts available, on many matters humanity, even highly intelligent humanity, indulges in emotional disagreements based not on the evidence available but on how individuals 'feel' about a particular issue after having been indoctrinated at an early age into a way of thinking. This applies particularly on issues where there is little, or no, real evidence. The supreme examples are the religions about which wars have been, and are being, fought. Many innocents have been, and are being, killed or maimed because adherents of a religion have emotional attachments to the tales told of the lives, the miraculous insights and the words of long dead prophets written well after their deaths and of doubtful veracity. There are many other examples.

An example of emotions being raised based on a doubtful basis is that it is humanity's burning of fossil fuels that has caused global warming and that this warming will be to the detriment of the globe on which we all depend. There is a widespread belief that $CO_2$ in very small quantities in our atmosphere is entrapping heat in a greenhouse effect. Many believe this is so and that it is destructive, despite the fact that there have been periods when the $CO_2$ in earth's atmosphere has been in much higher concentrations and that without $CO_2$ in the atmosphere life as we know it would not be possible. (See *"Global Warming – Climate Change"*) The accumulation of $CO_2$ from the burning of fossil fuels and rising temperatures from that increase is seen as completely negative, even though it is possible that there could be benefits such as that areas previously too cold to produce food will become useful and that plants will grow more productively. Greenland is becoming green again. The very fact of fossil fuels being available in areas now deserts or covered by seas indicates that the earth was a much different place when those fuels were laid down in very productive periods. On the other hand many believe that because our heat source, our sun, is going through an inactive sun spot period similar to the Maunder Minimum period of little sun spot activity in the 17th century, we are heading for a little ice age similar to that which followed the Medieval Warm Period. People get quite passionate about both these quite disparate possibilities when it is clear that there is not enough evidence to back either as the certain future. There are other beliefs about which people get passionate. Rising seas will swamp huge areas of land now in use. Old forests are the lungs of the earth, when they actually are nett producers of $CO_2$. It is new growth that absorbs $CO_2$. The ice caps will melt due to human interference with nature. The Great Barrier Reef will be destroyed. Experts who promote these theories happily fly about the world in aeroplanes producing $CO_2$, give lectures, and accept benefits from the public purse, to further their claims. Here in Australia we produce about 1.3% of the world's $CO_2$, so what we do will make only the smallest of difference even if carbon dioxide is causing rising temperatures, which might not be true, and which will have benefits as well as detriments, but we are committed to 'green' energy even though it is expensive and is not available at all times, because of emotional appeals by those who can benefit from its use, and a core of carbon evangelists.

Humanity should not allow itself to be swayed by emotions engendered by doubtful religions or doubtful theses, especially those religions that claim dominance over all, or those theses, such as global warming, that foretell doom brought about by the activities of us humans. We must use balanced logic and scientific measurement to arrive at our actions. To thrive, humanity must rid itself of its ancient urges for tribal dominance and realise that either we will all win or we could all be subjected to mutual destruction. Having said that, I do not hold out a great deal of hope for sense and logic to prevail. Some will insist that it is their duty to rid the world of people of a particular race or a religious belief they see as sacrilegious. Some will use religious beliefs to prosecute wars that have as their stated aim the need to force others into the path they see as the path of the righteous, but that are really being fought to show who is superior. Humanity must rid itself of its silly tribal instincts – it must grow up – but will it? Will the best among us work together to tackle the huge problems facing us on this limited globe, or will we just continue breeding until the human population is too numerous to be sustained by our limited globe? (See *"The Population Flood"*). The part of the human race that appears to believe it is its duty to rid the world of infidels is steadily increasing, and the human race itself is growing at such a rate that it is possibly reaching plague proportions. Will this continue? Or will we continue to produce garbage until the habitable parts of the Earth's surface and the seas are covered in it and we have used up our globe's finite natural resources? Will we allow the weaknesses of our human psyche to dominate our dealings with each other until there are outbreaks of terrifying violence, and huge destruction, or will we be able to develop a new set of commandments that will enable us to live together peacefully within the sustaining capabilities of our Earth – our home? Will we be intelligent enough to put ill-founded emotions to one side and not let them govern our conduct, or will we continue to make decisions based on our 'feelings', not on logic? Is there hope or must we despair?

## 47. EMPLOYMENT FOR PEACE.

To enable the human race to live reasonably and peacefully there must be several basic conditions. The more obvious of these are – pollution free air and water, sustaining and digestible food, ambient conditions that are neither too hot nor too cold, shelter from predators and control of fatal diseases. And, there are other less obvious, more subtle, necessities, that are to do with the psyche of we *Homo sapiens*, and that are rarely discussed. These include a reason for living (we do not want to admit that we might be only an unimportant blip on the development of life on Earth as the dinosaurs have been), outlets for our creative drives, a set of fair and understandable rules that are framed to encourage us, disparate beings, to live in reasonable harmony, chances to learn from others and from history – to be educated – and to think, opportunities to develop and to fulfil ambitions and, very importantly, fulfilling occupations that each considers to be worthwhile. I question whether this last need is given sufficient consideration in our present, urbanised civilisations.

The need for satisfying occupations for a peaceful community was recognised by the Pharaoh Djoser's vizier, Imhotep, over 2500 years before Christ was born. Once Djoser united Upper and Lower Egypt there was little to do after the crops were planted and before they needed harvesting. Prior to the uniting, the periods had been filled with battles. Imhotep put to work the unoccupied people building a mastaba, a burial tomb, for the Pharaoh, and it gradually grew into what became the Step Pyramid. Later Pharaohs took Imhotep's model and improved it. They produced the only surviving Wonder of the Ancient World – the Pyramids of Giza. Peace reigned while the pyramids were constructed.

Later, in Europe, in the Middle Ages – the 5$^{th}$ to the 15$^{th}$ centuries, the period following the collapse of the mighty Roman Empire and its civilisation – the requirement for activities for those not engaged in food production was taken over by the Roman Catholic Church. Its adherents were called on to serve the church and to live peacefully with their neighbours to achieve everlasting life in Paradise. One serving occupation was war. Crusades were fought. Another was the building of Cathedrals for the glory of God. These featured works of art – stained glass windows, fluted, hand crafted columns and pointed arches, pictures and statues of saints, mosaic floors and carved timber furnishings. They occupied the entire populations of towns and satisfied the urge of creativity. Such famed artists as Leonardo da Vinci and Michelangelo were involved.

Based on examples such as these it appears that humankind needs either wars or construction – destruction or creation – to occupy it. If this is so, and there are many other examples that could be brought out to back it, the world is, once again, at a T junction. To one side there is war and destruction, and to the other creative employment. The world needs to choose. Which is it to be?

There are now problems that leaders have to face, that were not considerations when weapons were not as destructive and poisonous as they now are. Leaders still have to make the choice between employing their followers on construction, on improving living conditions, on more sophisticated infrastructures, and on better buildings, or on killing and destruction. Now the spoils of war are not so attractive. Once the victors gained useful land, greater living room and the buildings constructed by the previous owners. Now what they will gain is devastated and polluted countryside and wreckage. War has now reached a stage of sophistication that there are no 'winners'. In the present wars in the Middle East the destructive power of the weapons being used is limited but they have been powerful enough to have almost completely destroyed Raqqa.

Given the power of the weapons available today, and the long lasting effects a nuclear war will have on our Earth, there does not appear to be any intelligent direction to take but for leaders to agree to do away with war and to use the energies of their populations in attempts to build a better world for the future. Despite this we still have leaders flexing their weaponry muscles and spending huge portions of the public purse, and public energy, on machines of war – armies with their complex tanks and rockets, navies with their incredibly complex aircraft carriers, their sophisticated submarines and their fighting craft, and the air forces with their expensive and technically advanced bombers and fighters many of which will be destroyed in a conflict. Many countries – the western democracies, the strong Asian countries and Russia – are all armed for war and flaunt their weaponry. The world should be concentrating on achieving the difficult aim of universal employment on peaceful development. Instead, it is spending incredible amounts of human intelligence and human energy on ever more sophisticated means of destruction. This is ridiculous.

My simple mind finds it incredible that not one of the world's western leaders – Trump, May, Merkel, Macron, or even Australia's temporary leaders, are attempting to achieve a peaceful world. Instead of attempting to arrive at a world without international strife, together with Xi, Putin and Kim, they flourish their arms. This is no way to achieve peace, universal prosperity and a better world. Our leaders must now stop acting as combatants and macho bullies, and change from their current tough guy stances, to facing, and acting on, the real problems of the world we share – overcrowding, a probable lack of satisfying employment, pollution of various types, and unfortunate human traits that lead to people treating each other badly. We need our leaders to display the better qualities of humanity, not the more reprehensible, and to work together to alleviate the world's problems – not to exacerbate them.

To summarise the position as I see it:
- Based on its history humanity needs challenging occupations. The two main possible branches of these occupations have been, until now – construction or destruction.

- In the past both approaches have been successfully employed by those leading various religious and secular groups. History is awash with various warrior leaders, some of whom are still lauded and some of whom are reviled.
- Our current world has several warlike leaders who are rattling their sabres so that those elements of the various societies who are peaceful have much to be concerned about.
- Past wars have led to the gaining of useful territory and property by the victors. But, given the poisonous nature of several of the weapons that will be used in desperate situations, winning useful areas is now unlikely. No-one will win if sarin gas is used or there is a nuclear holocaust.
- Given that weapons are now so destructive, and that damage from them is going to be so long lived, war is no longer an outlet for aggressive elements of humanity, if it ever was. War will destroy us all. It must be abandoned.
- In war's place peaceful outlets for humanity's energies must be found – outlets that are not destructive. What are the modern pyramids to be? Space travel? Mighty construction projects? Improved food production?
- Unfortunately the current crop of the world's leaders do not appear to have the qualities needed to overcome these very real problems facing us, or the ability to propose suitable constructive projects that will keep the growing world population happily and gainfully employed.

It appears the alternatives are that either the world's leaders change from their militant stances, and solve the real problems of how to lead us into peaceful and productive pastures, or our problems will escalate, and we could see the world around us destroyed.

## 48. HUMANITY'S STRENGTHS AND SHORTCOMINGS.

Where are humanity's strengths and weaknesses taking us? To destruction or to a peaceful and productive future? Humanity has evolved from a near Neanderthal like state to being the reigning species on the tiny planet Earth in the vastness of space. During its journey to its present state of development it has learnt to question and to think, it has studied the complexities of the human body and of space, it has constructed many impressive edifices and it has learnt to harvest nature for food, clothing and shelter. Humanity now ventures into the small section of space that is the Solar System and finds out more about our limited part of the total scheme of things. It studies the depths of the oceans and the microscopic world not available to the human eye. It develops complex theories and it harnesses nuclear reactions. It has learnt how to capture images and to transmit them. These are only some of the wonderful things humanity has managed to achieve. Members of the human race should be proud of its accomplishments. But are there downsides in humanity's developments?

We have not yet managed to eliminate many of the nastier traits we have inherited from our animal forebears. Why have we not? Why do many of us still squabble like bad tempered baboons? Why have we spent so much time and energy perfecting weapons that have the aim of killing enemy parts of the human species or destroying their creations? Why are there still those who consider parts of the human family to be inferior and are happy to wipe them out or to enslave them, when what we should all be attempting is to bring all up to the highest level possible? Why do so many of the world's leaders attempt to dominate instead of attempting to lead their followers to a healthier and more satisfying social ambience, and why does the mass of the population follow such leaders? Why do so many enthusiastically follow the myths of religions, especially religions that still seek to dominate by forceful violence? And why do so many humans exhibit greed and avarice when their short lives could be much more fulfilling if devoted to the welfare of humanity?

I understand and have experienced several of the forces that drive humanity and I also understand that many of these drivers fade with age so that it is easy for the aged – of which I, at eighty seven, am one – to be critical of those driven to dominate when that domination results in detriment to those dominated. This does not mean I am against competition, which can bring out the best in those competing. I am against competitions that can, or do, result in harm to persons or to destructive artefacts produced by human endeavour. This means that I am not against racing of any type, even though it can be dangerous, and I am not against gambling if it is freely entered into – although I do not gamble. I am against conflicts that can result in mutilation or death and do not understand the attraction of such conflicts. They appear to me to be a sad part of humanity's nature, a throwback to a violent past, and a weakness. Given the opportunity I would certainly ban combats aimed at maiming or killing, whether between humans, or between humans and animals. Contact sports such as some of the football codes, ice hockey, boxing and wrestling fall into no-man's land in my opinion. Some have advantages such as teaching teamwork and some let off steam that might be turned into more aggressive pursuits if not spent between consenting combatants.

What I do not understand is why the human animal, with its much vaunted intelligence, has not yet reached a universal conclusion that the killing or maiming of others, and the destruction of the creations of others, are crimes against humanity and should not be a part of a civilised world. As long as crimes of this type are being carried out there is the strong possibility that they will also be turned against those who initiate them. Surely it should be clear that making weapons of destruction is almost certain to see them being used and that it is infinitely preferable not to have them. The high intelligence and skills needed to make atomic bombs should, surely, be better employed for researching space, ascertaining the number of people the Earth can reasonably support, improving our means of construction, communication and mobility, finding out how to improve crop yields, overcoming some of nature's challenges such as fire, flooding and seismic movements and overcoming diseases that kill the vegetation and animals on which we rely and that can destroy individual humans. There appear to be more than enough challenges to occupy human intelligence without it being used to refine means of destruction. We also need tasks that provide satisfaction for those parts of humanity that do not have a scientific bent – for those with skills with animals, growing useful plants, caring for the ailing, constructing the accommodation and transport facilities so necessary in our modern world, creating things of beauty, maintaining law and order and, probably most important of all, educating the young in a balanced and wholesome manner devoid of reliance on destructive myths. Is it possible that humanity can develop such a world or is it that humanity is composed of inherently nasty creatures and that death and destruction is necessary to satisfy the make-up of a part, if not the whole, of humanity?

If humanity is to survive it is my view that it is vital that it overcomes its tendencies to squabble and rattle its sabres of destruction. America's and China's current showings of their armed might appals me. As the most powerful and successful nations on our speck of a planet, in our vast universe, it is time both showed some leadership and stopped showing off their armed and drilled armies, navies and air forces and concentrated on the long range health and well-being of humanity on our one and only Earth.

There are also the problems of some of the lesser nations – nations not yet developed to a level at which they fit into the world as it now is, with their leaderships apparently being intent on the leader's self-importance – not on the long term welfare of the citizens of the nation. The classic case is Kim

Jon-un of North Korea who has managed to alienate all peaceful parts of the world with his gleeful showing of his country's long range rockets, but there are others. Mugabe and Zuma of Africa were two until both were recently replaced, whether for the better remains to be seen at this time. Are other leaders of the African nations aiming at a peaceful world or are their motives personal power? If there are leaders in the Middle East who are intent on peaceful development we have not heard of them. I presume because peaceful people are not newsworthy. Peaceful leaders do not include Bashar al Assad of Syria about whom we hear a good deal as his followers make war and destroy. We hear much about militant leaders but nothing about Alain Berset. Who, I hear you ask, is Alain Berset? He was the President for 2018 of the peaceful country of Switzerland.

Surely it is time that the leaders that are selected are people who want peaceful cooperation, not people who insist on demonstrating how tough they are, as they shelter in their armed palaces and are surrounded by their armed guards. Unless the world changes and leaders are selected who are not interested in conquering but in finding solutions to the world's problems, encourage those able to uncover the mysteries of the Earth and its surrounds, and provide worthwhile tasks for those who are able and willing, the future appears bleak. Weapons capable of destroying life on Earth are now available.

## 49. EQUALITY.

For the human race there can be no such thing as equality of all members, because each member has different and unique physical, mental and psychological characteristics, and each exists in a unique environment. Although this is so, for the future welfare of humanity we humans should strive for equality of opportunity for all. This means we should try to provide the following necessities for all humans.
- Clean water and adequate food.
- Reasonable shelter from the elements.
- Rounded and balanced education free from superstitions and destructive biases.
- Opportunities for advancement that are as equal as possible.
- Encouragement of individuals to use and improve their talents and abilities for both their own advancement and the advancement of their society.
- A reasonable balance of financial rewards and a reasonable distribution of accolades for those who contribute to their society.

It will be important that humanity's societies maintain the driving force of competition and encourage personal ambition. My hope is that, in future, personal ambition will be aimed more at improving society's welfare by all individuals, instead of being aimed at personal power and wealth, as it now is by so many. To achieve a vital and competitive society the provision of public largesse will have to be carefully monitored. Sloth, which is destructive of the human spirit, must not be made enticing. Society should endeavour to ensure that huge financial success by manipulation of markets that should be free (both labour and financial markets), is not the main aim of its more able citizens.

It should always be borne in mind that real wealth is created from harvesting animals and plants, from mining and collecting useful elements from the surface and the near depths of the Earth (coal, oil, gas and various minerals and deposits), from making and manufacturing articles that have a market value, and from inspirations that lead to greater efficiency in the making or obtaining these wealth producers.

Whatever system is adopted, for us to live together in harmony, I consider it important that we treat all citizens equally. Does Australia do this – or does it treat some groups and individuals differently because of their religion, their ethnic background, their sex (or their sexual proclivities), their possession of, or lack of, physical attractiveness and their natural abilities? And do all Australians contribute to their society as best they can? For a morally healthy, prosperous and progressive society it is clearly necessary that all are given opportunities, and that as many as possible meet their duty to contribute to their society. Taking from your society is less rewarding than contributing to it.

One matter that needs to be settled as fairly as possible is whether a case can be made for treating some individuals or groups differently because their forebears were mistreated. Australian history contains several cases of minority groups having been treated badly.

Examples are:
- Afghan camel handlers, who opened up the centre of our wide, brown land with their camels, were treated harshly by the laws and societies of their time. They have left descendants who are proud of their heritage. Should they, today, be treated differently from other ethnic groups, should they be given special privileges, or should we just be grateful that they have melded into our general society?

- Over 100,000 Germans settled in South Australia early in the 20<sup>th</sup> century. They cultivated the land, planted wheat and established the Australian wine industry. Despite the fact that several of the young men enlisted to fight for Australia in the First World War, and that several died in action, many of the group were interned for the duration of the war and lost their businesses. This shabby treatment has not stopped the group from contributing to their society in many ways and they have not been given any special compensation for it.
- After the Second World War hundreds of displaced persons from the Baltic States came to Australia on assisted passages. They were called "Balts' and/or "New Australians". Some stayed in Western Australia and some went on to Wodonga, from where they were dispersed as labourers and domestics. All were obliged to work for two years to pay for their passages. Quite a number of the Western Australian contingent were sent to South Kumminin where families lived in tents and the men built and maintained railways. They served their terms and have since been absorbed into the general population. As far as I am aware they have received no special privileges since.

The point I hope I am making is that many minorities have been treated harshly and have become contributing citizens and part of their adopted country. They have prospered as the country has prospered.

Partly because of the history of these minority groups, and others, and because I believe that all citizens should be treated as equally as possible, I do not agree with special treatment being given to any racial group, including those with mixed lineages, and believe that by treating any racial group as mendicants and encouraging it to expect hand-outs instead of expecting it to contribute, that group is being degraded. I see no point in attempting to redress the past treatment of any group by providing special privileges to its descendants. I sincerely believe that those who do what they can to contribute to their society are happier and morally healthier than those who take from their society.

I do not understand why so many, otherwise healthy and apparently well balanced, Australians greedily take whatever they can from their society and regard amassing fortunes and assets as the best life choice. I, especially, do not understand why, what appears to be the bulk of Australians, seem to consider that it is their right, and a reasonable choice, to take as much as they can from the public purse and a much superior activity to contributing to that purse. This ethos of taking as much as possible and contributing as little as possible is not one that builds a great society. For a great society to be built requires that all contribute as well as they can – or am I being too sententious?

Getting back to equality. It is my view that to get as close to equality as possible it is necessary that there be equality of opportunity, and for equality of opportunity it is necessary that all have the following.

- A balanced and rounded education provided by intelligent and learned teachers who have no biases and present accurate information, including information about humanity's inhuman treatments of some groups now and in the past. Of course for education to be worthwhile it is necessary that the young want to learn. If there is resistance to learning, as there appears to be with some groups, those who resist are heading for a sad life as mendicants.
- No special benefits because of religious beliefs or ethnicity. For a society seeking equality no minority group should be favoured.
- As well as being educated in the normal subjects (reading, writing and mathematics) and the history of humanity, the young should also be given instruction in what constitutes reasonable behaviour and the reasons why it is better to behave morally. They should also learn that taking what has not been earned, or freely given, is destructive of the society in which they live, and of the well-being of those who steal and cheat.
- It is my view that education should also cover the main religions and the basic tenets of their beliefs – their similarities and their differences, their destructive wars and what proofs there are of the accuracy of their beliefs. They should be compared and each one not allowed to be fed to young minds as the only truth. Equality and balance cannot be achieved by educating the young in only one set of beliefs – especially the beliefs of a religion that believes enslaving and killing unbelievers is a holy task. It would be as well to include brief lectures on several of the lesser religions for balance.

I realise that many will not agree with my recipes for equality and will consider that their particular religion or their social mores should be adopted by everyone, and that if this is accomplished equality will be achieved. Given the history of the past this will not happen, and without broad and balanced education, religious and ethnic groups will continue to wage war. Because weapons of destruction are now so lethal, and their effects so long lasting, humanity must now strive for universal peace or we will destroy our only habitable home – our Earth. We must now stop the childish displays of our expensive weapons of destruction and expend our energies achieving universal education and well-being. There is no doubt in my mind that it is time to break away from the educational and religious systems that have led to conflicts in the past, and to spend our energies on peace instead of on weapons and fighting.

If there are other solutions to achieving equality and peace I want to hear them.

# 50. THE PURPOSE OF LIFE ON EARTH.

Since humanity started to think it has pondered the question of why we humans exist. The purpose of our lives has been at the forefront of our thinking. Most of us appear to have accepted that the huge number of living creatures – both animal and vegetable, that inhabit the surface and the oceans of the Earth – can be exploited by us (although Hindus will not kill cows). The belief that humans are special is universal and that our existence is, somehow, more important than that of other animals, even the closely related and intelligent animals. Even badly, mentally and physically, damaged human beings are considered to have special qualities. It is also widely believed that each human possesses an essence that the rest of the Earth's animals and vegetables lack, and that this essence continues on after we die. English speakers call this unproved essence a soul.

Around this unproven belief, that each human possesses an immortal soul, have been constructed many religions by various groups, at various times, in various parts of the world. The current big four are Hinduism, Christianity, Islam – the Moslem religion, and Judaism. Each of these religions believes that theirs is the only true religion and that only believers in that true religion will ascend to an everlasting and comfortable paradise. Given that all these religions are late arrivals in the 300,000 year history of we humans and that there have been many other religions with similar beliefs in life after death – the ancient Egyptians and the Norse Gods with their Valhalla are examples – it seems illogical to me that anyone can believe that an all-powerful God would reveal Itself to only one person, whether it was Moses, Jesus or Muhammad. These beliefs, in an everlasting soul, and an all knowing deity who corresponded with only one person, have no proof and cancel each other out. None can be the truth.

What the religions have done, that could be considered of benefit to humanity, is that they have laid down sets of rules that have to be followed if an everlasting life in Paradise is to be achieved. This means that large sections of humanity have been led to meeting the tenets of their religion to achieve a blissful afterlife – they have been controlled in their activities – which has led to different groups being disciplined in their actions, and that has led to peaceful development. What religions have also done, that could be considered detrimental, is to have gone in militantly different directions and to have had periods of corruption. The leading religions that have developed in the Middle East – Judaism, Christianity and Islam – and which are now nearly universal, are at loggerheads even today, and have been at war over the centuries. Their disagreements have led to appalling behaviour, especially by the Christian and Moslem religions, on many occasions. Judaism has not been viciously aggressive as the other two religions have, possibly because it lacked the strength of the others and perhaps because it has seen itself as superior and able to succeed by means other than through war. It certainly has used the high intelligence of its followers and their business acumen to control a good deal of the world's finance. The successes of its adherents has certainly caused followers of other religions to become jealous of the Jewish financial and scientific successes and to attack its followers. Adherents of the Christian religion followed Hitler into treating the Jews appallingly. Today the Christian religion is wilting in many parts of the world and is not attacking the widespread Jewish community but the Moslems are, and are attempting to remove the Jews from Israel by force and killing. The question is – how can humanity unite these warring parties into a universal whole that lives peacefully?

Perhaps the cycle of war and destruction followed by periods of peace and re-building is the inevitable lot of humanity as foreseen by George Orwell in his book *"1984"*. Perhaps our warring tribal instincts will continue to overcome our striving for peace.

What I think this all means is that before humanity can settle into investigating and solving the real problems of our one and only world, our planet Earth, we must do away with militant religions, and their calls to subdue those who do not follow that religion. The areas of research we should be pursuing are:

- Balanced education for all. First we must come to reasonable decisions as to what balanced education is. We must do away with brain washing the young.
- How and why life came into existence and whether or not it exists in other worlds.
- Finding the optimum population numbers that can be comfortably supported by our limited Earth and finding ways of keeping to those numbers.
- Finding challenges that will occupy the energies of the massive population so that peace will reign and good things will be done.
- Building ever better edifices, means of transport, communications systems and food producing farms.

Although I consider we must aim at doing away with religions generally it is the militant religions that concern me most. Some religions provide innocuous guiding lights for their followers and some humans, especially those indoctrinated when young, appear to need the comforts they provide. Such people will not be emotionally satisfied by the understanding that they are little different from other animals and that their lives are limited to their tenure on Earth. They need the comfort of a life after death.

The Muslim religion with its calls for striking off the heads of infidels, its dreadful treatment of women, and its promises of rewards for those who die in the cause of Allah is not a benign religion, and societies that accept it on the grounds of religious tolerance are taking a risk – a risk that was epitomised by the destruction of the architect, Minoru Yamasaki's, twin towers in New

York. I have met the gentle and creative Yamasaki and regard destruction of his towers, and the killing of thousands, to be crimes against humanity.

My own beliefs, based on logic and history is that life, including human life, is only an accident on our one and only Earth, that we are not important in the total scheme, that there is no deity taking note of all our actions, and that we should learn to live with these realities. We must realise that our energies should be directed towards pursuing peaceful objectives that will benefit humankind and that future destructive wars will detrimentally affect all humanity that is not slaughtered. War is no longer an activity for bad people and heroes, for fighting personnel and merciful medicos, and for the home front providing the fighting forces with what they need. War will now be horribly destructive and its effects long-lasting. We do not appear to have learnt anything from Nagasaki and Hiroshima.

Humanity now needs to realise that all races should be treated similarly, that it must abandon the ridiculous arms race that is now being conducted, and must occupy itself with learning, investigating and constructing things of value for the future. If it continues to act as warring tribes led by militant leaders such as Putin, Xi, Trump, Assad, the Saud family and the leaders of the threatening branches of both the Sunni and the Shia branches of Islam, all those living on the Earth and all those who will inherit it will suffer.

# 51. GLOBAL WARMING – CLIMATE CHANGE.

The IPCC, the Intergovernmental Panel on Climate Change, has reported that our Earth is warming and that we only have 12 years to prevent a climate change catastrophe by limiting global warming to 1.5°C. The IPCC puts the current rise, which it says is 1°C, down to anthropogenic activities – that is, to the activities of us humans. The IPCC believes that unless we limit our production of $CO_2$ our climate will change catastrophically, and there will be destructive rises in sea levels. The IPCC calls for huge reductions in our production of $CO_2$ but it, currently, does not appear to have a solution as to how to achieve this and still provide the electrical power, and transport facilities, our societies want except by 'renewables' which other research has found to be a questionable possibility. I am not surprised that the IPCC has found that there is a major problem and that unless we change our ways there will be a catastrophic rise in temperature and the coral reefs of the world will expire. Had the IPCC not found such problems they would not have justified the expense of their investigation and they would have had to have abandoned their well-paid and important positions. Before the world reacts to their findings there should be more investigation and more consideration as to how accurate they are and how, if the findings are caused by humanity as the IPCC suggests, whether or not the temperature rises are the disaster they are being made out to be. There are many imponderables. Research in Denmark by Henrik Svensmark questions the sensitivity of the climate to CO2 and suggests that cosmic rays and clouds affect the climate more than the level of CO2. Valentina Zharkova, at Britain's Northumbria University, believes a natural sun cycle will increase the Earth's temperature by 2.5°C. Researchers in Japan are questioning whether clouds cause a temperature rise, and have found evidence that cosmic rays create low clouds that then provide an umbrella, which leads to cooling. In Australia Michael Asten, a senior research fellow at Monash University has reported that scientists have barely scratched the surface of the task of recognising and modelling natural cycles of climate change. There is no consensus as to the contributions volcanoes – both those based on land and the many under the seas – make to the CO2 load and whether or not it exceeds the loading of us humans. Based on the wide spread of scientific opinion it appears humanity has some way to go before we understand climate change and can hope to control it.

There is no doubt that global warming – climate change is a matter of importance to the human race. It is raising the emotions of many, including the young, but only in western societies. Honourable people want to save our one and only Earth from overheating. In this paper I have attempted to provide some history and a balanced view on the matter of climate change. The paper also suggests that some of the approaches now being taken to curtail climate change could be expensively self-defeating and that positive steps could involve the human race in making sacrifices and reducing their numbers.

Based on our Earth's earlier history, a history that took place well before we humans evolved, it is clear that the climate has changed dramatically in the distant past without any interference from us humans. It is also clear that the climate has changed markedly fairly recently – as recently as history for which we have human records. Therefore it is more than likely that it will continue to change whatever we do. Whether the changes are detrimental or beneficial remains to be seen.

I am disturbed by those who protest, in many parts of the world, against humanity's burning of fossil fuels to produce electrical power unless they have studied the history of climate and understand it. I am particularly disturbed that the general Australian public and their children are being led to believe that they can help control climate change by using only 'renewable' energy. I am further disturbed by those who state, unequivocally, that the climate question is settled. It is not – as I hope to demonstrate. I am, however, somewhat heartened by the fact that some of the questions that needed to be asked before committing Australia to 'renewable' energy, are now being asked. And scientifically based papers that produce opinions that do not agree with the argument that climate change is due to anthropogenic activity are being presented that give reasons for their disagreement. (See William Kinnimont's paper *"The Ocean is a Brake on the Climate"*)

Do those who condemn the growing amount of $CO_2$ in our atmosphere realise that all plant life, and therefore all animal life, including us humans, depend on the approximately 400 parts per million (PPM) of $CO_2$ in today's atmosphere? Do they know that the concentration of $CO_2$ in Earth's atmosphere was as high as 4000 PPM in the Cambrian period about 500 million years ago? Have they learnt that the Cambrian period was followed by the Ordovician period (about 450 million years ago) when the Earth's climate cooled from warm and wet with very high sea levels, to a 20 million year ice age that created massive glaciers and the sea levels fell by about 80 metres? At that time, according to my computer, the $CO_2$ in the Earth's atmosphere has been measured as being at a level approximately 1500% higher than it is today. That our Earth froze when its atmosphere had, simultaneously, very high levels of $CO_2$ must throw some doubt on the theory that $CO_2$ is the main controlling agent of global warming.

Following the big freeze was the Carboniferous period (about 300 million years ago), during which the coal we now mine and burn was laid down by verdant forests. Those thriving forests absorbed $CO_2$ and exhaled oxygen until they affected further growth. The forests died out as the atmosphere ran low on $CO_2$ and the percentage of oxygen in the Earth's atmosphere, which is now 21%, rose to be 35%.

What investigations by clever geologists have found is that atmospheric conditions have never been static. Current $CO_2$ levels are at historically low levels but they are rising.

So much for our climate's ancient history. In more modern times our Earth has been subjected to the Roman Warm Period (RWP, AD100 –AD400) and the Medieval Warm Period (MWP, AD950 – AD 1250). During the MWP Eric the Red discovered, colonised and farmed a country he named Greenland. Grapes grew in middle England. The MWP was followed by the Little Ice Age (LIA, AD 1300 – AD1915) during which the colonisation of Greenland was withdrawn because the climate changed, Napoleon's invasion of Russia was routed, and his army destroyed, by freezing winter weather, and the river Thames regularly froze over.

According to Google the Intergovernmental Panel on Climate Change has been reticent about broadcasting the facts of the MWP and the LIA because they do not align with the IPCC's current position on global warming – that it is humanity's burning of fossil fuels and the resulting production of $CO_2$ that is causing global temperature rises – and will lead to catastrophic climate changes. History, both ancient history, and more recent, recorded history clearly shows that there have been huge variations in our Earth's climate. It also appears from history that warm periods are more productive than cold periods and are better for us humans. More of the Earth's surface becomes available for the production of foods, and oceans evaporate more so rain is likely to support plant growth.

Although global temperatures have not risen as much as the IPCC previously predicted – so that 'global warming' has become 'climate change'– there has been a rise in the level of $CO_2$ and a rise in temperature. There are several possible contributors to these rises.

They include:
- Variations in the sun's activities (sun spots, solar irradiance, solar magnetism)
- Variations in the tilt of the Earth's axis and its orbit around the sun.
- Volcanic activity, which leads to increases in the level of $CO_2$.
- Increases in the amount of water vapour in the atmosphere and clouds.
- As yet unknown factors that remain to be uncovered.
- Humanity and its activities (the increasing number of humans and the animals they nurture for food, the removal of plant life and its

replacement with inert areas, the continuing, and increasing burning of fossil fuels) which increase the output of CO2 and other greenhouse gases such as methane and nitrous oxide.

According to studies provided by Google, in the past the Earth's global temperature has closely followed the sun's Total Solar Irradiance (TSI). Despite this, some scientific opinion now appears to be that the sun's activities have only a minor effect and that the prime cause of 'climate change' is human activity. Based on ancient history the percentage of CO2 in the atmosphere is low, but it is rising. Whether this will lead to catastrophic weather changes or to more productive and pleasanter conditions for humanity – as it did in the Medieval Warm Period – only time will tell.

Because they have been influenced by frightening predictions that rising temperatures will prove destructive, there are many ordinary people in the comfortable western world, and that includes Australians, who believe that it is the duty of humanity to reduce the level of CO2 being created. This will affect the Australian manufacturing industry, which is already suffering from high electricity costs. It will be made less competitive, than it already is, by banning the production of electrical power by burning fossil fuels, of which Australia has an abundance. Because Australia has a small population of 26 million (about 0.35% of the world's total population of 7.6 billion) it produces only a very small percentage of the world's CO2 (about 1.3 – 1.4%), so that even if we stopped production of CO2 completely it would not affect the world's production of a gas that is necessary for plant life.

If the level of CO2 in our atmosphere is as important as it is being made out to be, then its many sources of production and its absorption by land plants and the oceans must be analysed. Before we make decisions that affect our economy and our way of life we need to know what is producing CO2 and other greenhouse gases and what takes nourishment from those gases. We must also attempt to ascertain whether CO2 is as damaging to the Earth's climate as has been assumed given that several scientists consider that water vapour and clouds have a much greater 'greenhouse' effect than CO2 and these are not now controllable. According to Wikipedia water vapour and clouds are the main contributors to the greenhouse effect, being responsible for between 36% and 72% of the effect. As the world heats up it is likely that the level of water vapour and cloud in the atmosphere will increase as the oceans evaporate faster so their contribution to global heating could increase.

If water vapour and clouds are the most important greenhouse effect contributors the next most important is said to be $CO_2$, which is responsible for 9% to 26% of the effect. How these percentages are arrived at I do not know but they are widely accepted. The contributions that stem from humanity's activities are:

- The production of electrical power from the burning of fossil fuels. According to Wikipedia this is responsible for 25% of the $CO_2$ produced by humans. It is this contribution of $CO_2$, on which those who assume it is humanity's activities that are leading to global warming, have concentrated. They want 'renewables' to produce electrical energy and to run vehicles and industry on that energy. As the production of electrical power is responsible for only 25%, or so of the world's total production of $CO_2$, it appears to me that if it is humanity's production of $CO_2$ that is the prime cause of global warming, producing electrical power by renewables is not going to overcome the global warming problem, if there is one. As the three greatest emitters of $CO_2$ from the production of electrical power – China, the USA and India – are not going to cut their emissions, I consider that Australia should not be attempting to cut theirs if the cut affects its economy. There is no doubt that electrical power is necessary for pleasant and productive living on our globe so that if burning fossil fuels is the prime cause of global warming we will have to find another means of economically producing that power.
- Our Earth is crowded with humans and other living creatures that service those humans and provide food. All breathe and exhale $CO_2$ and methane. Just what the productions of $CO_2$ and methane of the 7.6 billion humans and the animals that provide them with hides, wool, milk and meats are I do not know, but they would be substantial and are increasing as the population of the world increases. Is the production of

CO2 by humans and their animals so great that we should be considering the means by which the numbers living on our finite globe can be reduced? This is never discussed by those who want our production of CO2 to be reduced or by our political leaders.

- There are now many forms of transport that burn fossil fuels. The world is awash with motor vehicles – cars, buses, tanks, trucks – for transporting passengers and freight and for making war. There are large and small ships for transporting holidaying humans and freight around the world and, once again, for making war. Our skies are loaded with aeroplanes carrying passengers and armed for war. There are now, also, rockets burning fuels to explore space, to take modules into orbit and to show the might of the countries that have proudly produced them. On the ground there are trams and trains, many of which are propelled by electricity produced by burning fossil fuels (except in France – nuclear powered, and Norway – hydraulic energy powered). Transport is a major emitter of CO2. Is it possible that, in future, fossil fuels for our means of transport can be replaced by renewable energy or should we be changing our life styles so that we need less reliance on transport?
- Then there are the luxurious life styles to which humans aspire with our large houses, our many cars, our imposing city buildings constructed from materials that require a great deal of energy – concrete, steel, aluminium, glass, tiles, bricks and plastics – and all of which require heating, cooling, ventilation, lighting, internal transport systems and electrically powered communications and safety systems.
- If we are serious about limiting CO2 we must consider our wasteful modes of living, our freedom of travel and our many wars. Should we not be considering how we can avoid sitting in lines of traffic in every city in the world with our motors idling and spewing out CO2 and nitrous oxide? Should we all stop taking unnecessary aeroplane trips both nationally and internationally? Is it now time to change our wasteful life modes and revert to lower key and simpler life styles? Or are we wedded to our present life styles and greater exploitation of our Earth's produce until we foul our home?

Back to Australia. As I have previously reported Australia is responsible for about 1.3 – 1.4% of the world's $CO_2$ so we have almost no effect on any change in the world's climate that gas might, or might not, make. Many thoughtful Australians consider that our contribution is so small that we do not need to cut our emissions, especially as the major contributors – China, the USA and India – are not cutting theirs. They do not want to cost us out of the world markets. It is quite foolish of leaders such as Bob Brown and Richard Di Natale of the Greens to suggest that the Great Barrier Reef can be saved by Australia abandoning using fossil fuels for transport and the production of electricity when the major contributors are actually increasing their outputs of what, almost certainly, is a gas beneficial to plant growth. They are appealing to emotion, not to scientific fact, as they should be.

There are other considerations. Australia's contribution to $CO_2$ production is much greater than the fossil fuels we burn in Australia. Australia is now the world's leading exporter of coal, most of which goes to south-east Asia, and we are a major exporter of iron ore and industrial gas. Exported coal gained us revenue of $57 billion in 2017, gas gained us $25 billion and iron ore and concentrates gained us $63 billion. Without these incomes, which contributed over $5000 for each citizen of Australia, the Australian economic position would be even worse than it is. Fossil fuels are propping up our standard of living. Turning our exported iron ore into steel creates a major output of $CO_2$. If we believe that $CO_2$ is causing climate change then we must realise that we are contributing to its rise in our atmosphere to boost our economy. There is a saving grace. If we did not provide high grade coal to China and India it is likely they would use more polluting coals from other sources.

I find it strange that we are exporting the iron ore, and the coal to smelt it, to China when, given that there are major costs in transporting both, it should be more economical and would produce less $CO_2$ if the steel was produced here. Why do those who believe that $CO_2$ is going to make living on our Earth more hazardous not criticize this waste?

As can be seen, the picture of $CO_2$'s increase in our Earth's atmosphere, for good or ill, the contributions from its various sources and its effects on Australia's finances, is a complex one. Industries in many parts of the world, including Australia, depend on the unpopular means of producing electricity by burning fossil fuels or from nuclear energy.

Those who take an interest in the science behind the globe's climate, and it is doubtful that they are a greater proportion of the Earth's population than those who ignore it, are concerned that the world's climate is changing in a manner that is detrimental to humanity and believe that humanity can control the change by producing less $CO_2$. Their concerns have been fuelled by Al Gore's films and the IPCC. But will a warming Earth bring nothing but disaster? Will a repeat of the Medieval Warm Period (which was followed by the Little Ice Age) be disastrous for us who live on the Earth or will Greenland bloom again? These questions have not been asked or answered. The global warming press has been a story of only disaster.

Those concerned that a warm period will be harmful to humanity have selected the burning of fossil fuels to propel vehicles and to produce electrical power as their prime targets despite the fact that water vapour and clouds are the main causes of the greenhouse effect. These well intentioned people believe that by producing electrical power by, so called, 'renewables' the production of $CO_2$ will be stemmed and our Earth will be saved from further heating. Before humanity's production of electrical power is handed over to these expensive 'renewables' I think further investigation and unemotional discussion needs to be undertaken and unemotional decisions taken.

Given that there have been previous warm periods and periods of chill earlier in the Earth's history is it possible, or even likely, that it is beyond humanity's ability to control such events? Is it possible that it is not $CO_2$ that is causing rising temperatures, and that the rising percentage of $CO_2$ in the atmosphere is following the rising of the temperature, not leading it – as believed by many? Do we need to know more of the effects – both the good effects as well as the bad – of a rise in the global temperature before we make decisions that will bring discomfort and cost to our world and that we could, later, find that we humans, cannot control the climate anyway? Even if it is possible for us humans to limit the output of $CO_2$, and even if time proves that the rise in global temperature can be controlled by that limitation, it will require all nations to adopt a $CO_2$ free approach. Without China, the USA,

India, Europe and Japan cutting their emissions what the rest of the world does is irrelevant.

According to the Union of Concerned Scientists the main producers of CO2 in 2015 were China (9,040 million metric tonnes), the USA (5,000 m.m.ts), India (2,060 m.m.ts), Russia (1,470 m.m.ts) and Japan (1,140 m.m.ts). I cannot vouch for the accuracy of these figures and I have no idea how they were calculated. What I do know is that unless these major contributors cut their omissions, and several have indicated they do not intend to do so, expensive 'renewables' efforts in Australia – 'renewables' that have led to failures of supply, as they did in South Australia – might be gallant but they are pointless. Should a very minor emitter such as Australia be attempting to cut its emissions, as promised by the Labor Party, when the major emitters are continuing to increase their emissions?

Should we continue to concentrate mainly on the emission of CO2 and cut its production when other greenhouse creators – methane, nitrous oxide, ozone and, especially water vapour and clouds – are also contributing?

One of the major shortcomings of renewable electrical energy is that it is not necessarily available on demand (as nuclear produced electrical energy is) so that storage is necessary for periods when the wind is not blowing, the sun is not shining and the seas are flat. This means that when renewable electrical energy is being tested against other forms of its production, the life costs and the energy sink of the necessary storage batteries has to be taken into account. In my research I have found nothing on the cost, longevity, capacities or disposal problems of storage batteries. I cannot understand why such basic information is not readily available. Before committing to a renewable system we must know how much storage batteries cost, how big they need to be, how they have to be housed, how long they will last, how they can be disposed of without affecting the environment and – most importantly – how much energy is absorbed in making, maintaining, dismantling and disposing of them.

Before we commit to more 'renewables' we must ascertain several things – things that have been hidden by government subsidies, and because there has been a lack of information provided. The primary matters are how much energy is required to fabricate, construct and maintain a renewable during its working life, and how much energy is required to demolish the unit and dispose of its debris at the end of its life? To this total must be added the energy required to make, install and maintain the batteries necessary to provide power when necessary and the energy needed for their demolition and disposal. This grand total of energy must be compared to the energy that will be delivered throughout the unit's useful life. Unless renewables can produce many times the energy necessary for their operation they are of doubtful worth because they, also, environmentally affect the areas in which they are built. Wind towers are being accused of killing birds and bats, some are already failing in Germany and others are being abandoned. I cannot understand why the energy required to make, operate and demolish renewables has not been compared to their lifetime's outputs and the results widely published. It is a basic requirement for making decisions as to their worth. A paper written by P. J. Ward in 2005, that examined the energy required to pay back the energy needed to build a wind tower, found that it would take 9 years to achieve that repayment – and that was without considering the energy required for connecting the tower into the power grid or for making and maintaining the necessary batteries. An English engineer involved in building wind towers told me that a good tower produced its energy input in 6 years but that an average tower took much longer – and that was without any allowances being made for maintenance, for demolition and disposal of the towers or for back-up batteries.

There has been little published information on the basic matter of the efficiency of batteries and their useful lives. How long will they last, and what is to be done with their remains? Are the remains readily recyclable? What energy is required for their demolition and disposal? Can they be easily, safely and readily disposed of? There has also been little information published on the energy produced by wind towers and PV cells during their working lives and comparisons made of that energy and the energy absorbed in making and maintaining these 'renewables'. Early PV cells have now reached the ends of their working lives and their demolition and disposal have problems. Only their aluminium frames can be melted down and re-used. The cells themselves are unfriendly detritus. The same question that besets nuclear power applies to the cells and to wind towers – what is to be done with this 'renewable' rubbish at the ends of its useful lives?

Although there are many who believe that renewables can replace other forms of power production economically there are critics. The Swiss engineer Ferrucio Ferroni and his partner Robert Hopkirk have been investigating Energy Return on Energy Invested (ERoEI) for photovoltaic (PV) solar systems. Their investigations show that the ERoEI is less than 1 for PV systems operating north of Switzerland. They are energy sinks. The ERoEI for wind turbines is not clear, as I consider it should be. A good deal of energy goes into making the towers, the blades, their working parts and their large, concrete foundations. I understand, but am not sure, that unless the ERoEI is in the region of 5 wind turbines with their maintenance costs, their necessary battery storages and their demolition and disposal costs are not financially, or practically, viable. They do have noise and environmental impacts. I noted during a recent trip through Germany that approximately one tower in every ten was stopped. The ERoEI for wind towers needs to be investigated by experts with no financial interest in turbines or their technology. Why it has not yet been done and broadcast I do not know, but the very fact that it has not is a concern.

An aspect of the drive for electrically powered vehicles that does not appear to have been given the necessary attention is whether or not the existing power distribution systems will be able to meet the demands that will be made on them. Systems are already under stress in several parts of Australia – both main power systems and local systems that have not been designed for such added loads. Major apartment buildings have not been designed to have charging stations at each parking bay and their transformers and power distribution systems were not designed for the loads that many vehicles being charged at once will require. It has been said that the cost to replace existing systems will dwarf the cost of the NBN system of over $50 billion. This needs proper analysis before we commit to electric vehicles.

There are many who consider that the current rise in the level of $CO_2$ in our atmosphere is due, mainly, to human activities and that it is leading to the rise in temperature that is occurring, not that it is following the rise in temperature as it has in the past. According to Google the main humanity emitters of CO2 are the provision of electricity (25% - 30%) and humanity's use of transport (approximately an equal amount according to the Environmental Protection Agency of the USA). I presume that the remaining 40% to 50% is produced by industry, fires, and respiration. Of humanity's production of CO2 it appears that somewhere about 50% of the current total production – the share produced by providing electrical power and from transport powered by internal combustion engines – is the maximum that can be saved by producing all electrical power from renewables. Political promises of zero emissions of CO2 are not possible and savings of 50% are only possible if it is confirmed that renewable sources of electrical power are truly viable.

To Summarise:

- There is little doubt that the concentration of CO2 in the Earth's atmosphere is rising. Whether this is due to rising temperature or whether it is primarily due to human activities, especially the burning of fossil fuels, is not agreed but the preponderance of scientific opinion is that we humans have caused the temperature rise, even though the Earth's temperature has varied widely in the past without any input from humans.
- Studies have shown that the Earth's climate has changed radically in the distant past and has changed markedly in the recent past without the burning of fossil fuels having contributed to the changes. History shows that warmer periods, such as the Medieval Warm Period, have generally been beneficial for humanity, so that a warmer period with higher concentrations of CO2, which benefits plant growth, could, again, be beneficial.
- Those who consider that climate change is a problem for humanity also appear to believe that it is possible to control that change by controlling the output of CO2. But it is water vapour and clouds that have the greatest greenhouse effect. This is not discussed. It is unlikely that evaporation can be brought under control by humanity.
- Even if it is CO2 that is the main agent of global warming and even if it is possible to control climate change by limiting humanity's production of the gas it will require all peoples to agree to only producing electricity by renewables and to use only electrically driven vehicles and machines.

I consider that it is very clear that this will not happen until destructive changes in the climate become obvious to all. As China, the greatest emitter of CO2, will not agree to limiting its production of CO2, except for token actions, and as China is increasing its output of CO2 each year by an amount greater than Australia's output, for Australia to cut its emissions to zero is a Quixotic gesture unless it can be done economically.

- Those committed to reducing the output of CO2 have, so far, concentrated on the production of electricity by renewables, and using that CO2 free power for its normal uses and to drive all vehicles, thus doing away with burning fossil fuels. The renewables being championed are solar powered photovoltaic panels (PVs) and wind towers. There are problems with these sources of electrical power. They are intermittent so they cannot respond to demand. They must have storage systems. Both they, and their batteries, have limited lives and lose efficiencies as they age. They will become obsolete and require replacement and demolition, as do other power producers. How long they will remain operationally efficient has to be found. Currently some early PV cells are being dismantled.
- The matter of the Energy Return on Energy Invested (ERoEI) of the popular 'renewables' – PV cells and wind towers – is not yet clear. That the return is much greater than the energy required to put these renewables into action and to store their outputs, needs to be clarified. This line of investigation needs further unbiased investigation by experts who have no axe to grind, and who will not profit from either the purveyors of fossil fuels, of those involved in renewables or those with interests in nuclear energy.
- Even if Australia spends time, effort and money on 'renewables' it is possible that it will not completely stem its production of CO2. It will still need some base load power plants and it will still be flying aeroplanes, driving some vehicles with internal combustion engines and powering ships and submarines with fossil fuels.
- Germany has hundreds of wind towers but it is still receiving electrical power from France's nuclear power stations and it is thinking of returning to producing some nuclear power itself.

It appears that there are many doubts about Australia committing to expensive, renewable producers of electrical power. Even if Australia is able to reduce its emissions of $CO_2$ to zero it will make only the slightest difference to the world's output. The Energy Return on Energy Invested for PV panels and wind towers, both of which require massive battery back-up, must be clearly in their favour before they are committed to. The fact that these figures are not already readily available and that Ferrucio Ferroni has found that PV panels can act as energy sinks should give rise to concern that renewables are not necessarily the panacea they are being made out to be by their purveyors.

If, as I consider the evidence indicates, full and balanced analyses of renewables has not yet been undertaken, they should be. Such analyses must take into account:

- Their lifetime absorption of energy for their construction and maintenance
- The energy required for their demolition and disposal once they have reached the ends of their useful lives and how their disposal can be safely made.
- The energy required for constructing and maintaining the battery systems that must support them and the energy necessary for their demolition and disposal.

If balanced analyses show that the 'renewables' and their batteries are not the panacea that those involved in their production have led the world to believe other means of producing electrical power that is flexible to demand, economical and $CO_2$ free will have to be used, if experience shows that $CO_2$ is, indeed, the prime cause of global warming.

So what are the alternatives for the future?

- The main emitters carry on the present outpouring of $CO_2$ in the beliefs that plants, both on land and in the seas, will flourish and absorb the excess as they did in the carboniferous period and that increases of $CO_2$ follow rises in temperature, not that they cause the rise. It should be remembered that it is water vapour that is the main greenhouse gas and that unless the main $CO_2$ emitters – China, the USA, India, Russia, Europe and Japan – can be persuaded to cut their $CO_2$ emissions what

the rest of the world does is nearly irrelevant.
- Improve our 'renewables' so that the energy consumed by their construction, maintenance, demolition and disposal, and their cost outlays are more than covered by their outputs. If they can show energy efficiencies, and that they are cost effective, they will proliferate without any handouts from tax payer funded governments. Governments providing taxpayers funds for trials is reasonable. Providing government funds for large inefficient systems is not.
- Change the lifestyles of the bulk of the world's populations. Cut the untrammelled use of electrical power for artificial climate control, the freedom of travel by aeroplanes, road vehicles and ships, and revert to a local village mode of living.
- Become more peaceful and stop our ridiculous warring. Our news is loaded with people, mainly men, controlling vehicles – trucks, armoured cars, tanks, fighter planes, bombers, submarines and warships spewing out $CO_2$ – and trying to kill each other. If these warriors could be persuaded to put down their arms and work to produce wealth – grow edibles, make useful implements, mine useful materials, build necessary infrastructures or educate the young, the world would be a better place and it would produce less $CO_2$. Is there any hope of this happening?
- Reduce the human population and the number of animals that support them. All humans and animals eat, respire and produce $CO_2$ and methane. Perhaps we should be considering attempting to control the birth rates of humans and their farm animals. The human population is now growing at a rate of 80 million each year, mainly in Africa and southern Asia. Is this sustainable?

Humanity must make one or more of these difficult choices. I hope it makes sensible choices that lead to peace and prosperity for most of the world's population. If populations continue to increase in number and the different tribes, religions and races continue to act militantly towards each other the result could be the annihilation of most, if not all, of the human race.

It is time that humanity recognised that we all have to live together in peace, and live within the productive capacity of our Earth, or we could destroy our one and only habitat. For productive peace we need much more than the puny change of Australia wasting time, effort and money on the CO2 savings that it can make.

## 52. ARE HUMANS IMPORTANT?

Nearly all Earth's creatures and plants live their lives as best they can without searching for a reason for their existence and without considering they are entitled to an everlasting life in a paradise. They just exist. The single exception is *Homo sapiens*. For some, illogical, reason we humans are quite satisfied to believe that pine trees, vipers, cucumbers, hippopotamuses and bed bugs are all temporary and have been created to live and die, having fulfilled roles in the existence of we humans, but that *Homo sapiens* (or, at least, selected parts of *Homo sapiens*) has been given the blessing of everlasting life by the powers that created the universe.

Since quite early in humanity's development it has searched for reasons for its existence. These searches have resulted in beliefs that there are supreme powers that have created the planet Earth and all its living creatures. Many *Homo sapiens* believe that these supreme powers have to be pandered to and worshipped. Some groups have developed beliefs that their lives have been granted to them so that they can follow laws laid down by their particular God – and there have been, and still are, many Gods.

According to Hindu beliefs there are 30 million Gods. Many of the Gods worshipped by ancient tribes are now forgotten. Consider the many Gods of the Druids, the extensive Inca God list, the 200 Gods of the Aztecs and the 12 major Norse Gods. The Encyclopaedia of Gods says that there are over 2,500 deities. The vast number of Gods that have been worshipped is clear evidence that we humans have been searching for reasons for our existence for many, many years and have settled on creation by Gods as an answer. But what is the chance of any one of the many religions being the only truth? Based on the evidence available it is my considered opinion that no all-powerful and loving God would have allowed such a mess, so that following of any one of the religions is wasting emotional energy.

The problem is – without a comfortable religion and a happy afterlife what is the point of human life? If instead of believing that if we follow the reported teachings of long dead men, (Note – not women – men! Why men?) we will reach paradise for eternity, we, *Homo sapiens*, believe that we are only another, unimportant, life form – a life form that could be wiped out as the dinosaurs were wiped out – we would have to arrive at new reasons for living comfortably together and face new challenges.

The supreme challenge that faces us is our continuing survival on our finite Earth. Currently, the leaders of the more powerful countries, instead of concentrating on how our disparate tribes, with their disparate beliefs, can live in peace and harmony for mutual benefit, they flaunt their destructive armaments – armaments that are now capable of making our Earth uninhabitable.

While the leaders of powerful economies rattle their weapons in shows of power the world quietly goes about piling up rubbish, a good deal of which is poisonous and long lived. As the powers of the monotheistic religions fade the religion of many becomes – what can I get and how can I get it? This naive greed will eventually lead to our one and only planet Earth accumulating rubbish and being divested of its usable plants and other usable, natural attributes unless humanity monitors and controls the use of finite resources.

We humans must stop militant posturing, those ages have passed, and now take up the following challenges.

- For the future well-being of humanity it is an absolute necessity that the young receive balanced education that not only equips them with the tools of being able to read, write and handle numbers, but that also provides a balanced history on the past actions of we humans and of the religions, their virtues and their terrible conflicts. Until humanity gets rid of militant religions the world can never be at peace.

- We must decide what the optimum populations are of both people and of the animals that support them, so that our production of greenhouse gases stabilizes and the consumption of food of various types does not exceed the balanced production of supply.
- How can *Homo sapiens* be persuaded to change from the irritable, argumentative creature it has been to a creature that realises that we need to all live together in peace or we could destroy our Earth – our home? We must stop our arguments, learn from the destructive parts of our history and all work together for a peaceful future.
- We must organise our civilisations for optimum living conditions; conditions that minimise our use of power of all types.
- We, disparate humans with our different skin colours, our varying histories, our varying moral, ethical, educational and religious backgrounds, and our differing temperaments must learn to live together for the welfare of all. Will we be able to achieve this given our history of conflict?
- Having noted that we humans have differing temperaments this could be the biggest stumbling block for a peaceful Earth. There are those who enjoy conflict, those prepared to kill, those who consider their religion important enough to force others to join it and those who consider themselves important enough to take wealth from others who have earned it, without having earned the right to do so. Will it be possible to change these destructive natures? Will those who have been predators be willing to receive balanced education that will change their natures and that will convince them that destructive activities will undermine the community in which they live? Will education change people with destructive natures, so that they will learn that destructive activities can destroy a community? Will they be prepared to learn that for the health of their community, and for their own health, it is necessary to be

providers, not predatory takers? Or is it not possible to change natures and is the dream of a balanced and peaceful population an impossible dream?

Probably the most important lesson that humanity must learn for future peace and prosperity is that its existence is an accident and that it is only a temporary phenomenon in the multi-million year history of the universe. It is not important in the total scheme of things. Humanity has now reached such a stage of knowledge and sophistication that it is capable of destroying life on Earth. Unfortunately it does not appear to have left its ancient stupidities and biases behind it yet. Will *Homo sapiens* learn and prosper, will it drown itself in garbage or will it destroy itself in a fit of stupidity?

## 53. ONLY ONE WORLD.

It is beyond my limited comprehension to understand why the leaders of humanity's many nations appear not to have reached the obvious conclusion that as there is only one Earth, the various human groups who inhabit it have no alternative but to find ways of living on it peacefully and cooperatively. We cannot continue to squabble and kill each other because our weapons of destruction – our poison gases and our nuclear weapons – are now so destructive and their poisons so long lived that from an all-out conflict there will be no victors. We humans must find ways of living together, and living within the productive capacities of our Earth, our home, or all humanity will suffer. I find it appalling that instead of our leaders spending their mental energies and time attempting to find ways to peaceful cooperation, they flaunt their armed might – their destructive capacities – much as a warrior chieftain of the stone-age would have done. Our leaders, however they have been selected, should have as their primary objective the means by which we can live together constructively, without ruining our globe. If there are leaders who strive to arrive at peaceful solutions to the overriding problem of human survival on our limited globe, they do not get a widespread press. I have not heard any leader from a powerful country state that peaceful cooperation is a necessity. Instead the leaders of the powerful countries continue to flaunt their destructive powers to other power blocs with different political systems, racial features or religions. It is past time to stop such foolish, rooster-like posturing, and to apply our best mental energies to arriving at the means for us to live peacefully together, and prosper. Either we find ways of living in harmony, or we will destroy our home. Either the days of armed conflict between the various ethnic and religious groups have to be put behind us, and we then cooperate to arrive at ways of living within the Earth's productive capacities, or we resort to further destructive, armed conflict – conflict from which there can be no winners. From a nuclear conflict, or the spreading of poisonous substances, there will be only losers.

So what are the steps that are necessary to achieve a peaceful and cooperative world? The most important is that the leaders we select must be those whose interests are the future welfare of humanity and our globe – not those whose aims are personal aggrandisement or in proving that their ethnic group, political system or religion, is superior to all others. Their aims must be the advancement of humanity, and the protection of our Earth. They must understand that humanity needs world-wide cooperation, or it is doomed. Our chosen leaders must not encourage research into ever more destructive weapons, as so many now do. They must encourage research into the best uses and husbandry of the Earth's resources, and how population numbers can be limited to figures that the globe can sustain.

Another important step is that religions that encourage spreading by force or indiscriminate breeding have to be done away with. I see no way that this can be accomplished except by educating the young on the shortcomings, the inhumanities, the nasty histories, and the distortions of the forceful religions. It is certain that the leaders of these religions will defend them, and resist any attempt at re-education, as his priests resisted Pharaoh Akhenaton's attempt to change to a single deity over 1300 years before Christ was born. Unless religions that encourage the death and destruction of non-believers are removed completely, there can be no peace. A way of getting into the minds of the followers of the forceful religions has to be found, or the young have to be given a balanced education. As any reader who has already read *"Religions"* is aware, it is my view that for the future of humanity all religions should be abandoned, but as so many decent people, people who live peaceful and productive lives, find solace and strength in religions that are concerned with peaceful and helpful activities, and do not proselytize forcefully, they should be allowed to continue until they die out naturally. I agree with Karl Marx that *"Religion is the heart of a heartless world and the soul of soulless conditions. It is the opium of the people"*. (This has also been translated as the opiate of the masses).

I consider it better to have that section of the population who desires it, to be pleasantly drugged by a peaceful and supporting religion than having them unhappy and unsure. However I am wholeheartedly against any religion that considers it is God's chosen, and that it is a duty to its God to destroy other religions and atheists.

Given humanity's track record, and the nature it has exhibited over many centuries, is it even remotely possible that leaders with the necessary characteristics will stand for leadership roles and, even if they do present themselves, will they be granted sufficient power to bring about the necessary changes? Will the Mugabes, the Assads, the Kims, the Trumps, the Xis and the Putins of our world willingly relinquish their powers to humanitarian thinkers, and would the electorates hand power to people with the necessary knowledge, ethos and character?

It is my view that unless the world reforms, unless by far the bulk of humanity gives up its murderous and destructive tribal and racial instincts, and decides to live peacefully in harmony with other parts of humanity, and within the productive capacity of the Earth, there will be further wrangling that will finally result in a holocaust, probably a nuclear holocaust, that will kill many, if not all, and will make much of our precious Earth uninhabitable. Humanity could repeat the fate of the dinosaurs.

To achieve the necessary changes in humanity's instincts and performances will require balanced education. But will people want to learn balanced views, or will they prefer to continue with their dreams of superiority, and of a privileged life after death?

I have been called a pessimist by some who consider that humanity will find a way through the problems that face it. I hope they are correct. Regardless of whether I am a realist or a pessimist I cannot see any reason not to discuss the problems I have covered as unemotionally as possible. I consider that the present situation of the world's leaders all, happily, showing the destructive power of their armed forces, and not one suing for peace and suggesting abandoning the current arms races, to be an indictment of our current systems of leadership selection and our stupidity in following militant leaders.

www.ingramcontent.com/pod-product-compliance
Lightning Source LLC
Chambersburg PA
CBHW080356030426

42334CB00024B/2899